21ˢᵗ CENTURY SOLDIER

21ˢᵀ CENTURY SOLDIER

The Weaponry, Gear, and Technology of the Military in the New Century

Frank Vizard and Phil Scott

ISBN: 1-931933-16-2
Library of Congress Control Number: 2002109643

21ST CENTURY SOLDIER: THE WEAPONRY, GEAR, AND TECHNOLOGY OF THE MILITARY IN THE NEW CENTURY

TIME INC. HOME ENTERTAINMENT
President: Rob Gursha
Vice President, Branded Businesses: David Arfine
Executive Director, Marketing Services: Carol Pittard
Director, Retail & Special Sales: Tom Mifsud
Director of Finance: Tricia Griffin
Associate Director: Peter Harper
Prepress Manager: Emily Rabin
Associate Book Production Manager: Jonathan Polsky
Special thanks: Suzanne DeBenedetto, Robert Dente, Gina Di Meglio, Anne-Michelle Gallero, Natalie McCrea, Jessica McGrath, Mary Jane Rigoroso, Steven Sandonato, Bozena Szwagulinski, Niki Whelan.

POPULAR SCIENCE
Editor in Chief: Scott Mowbray
Design Director: Dirk Bennett
Science Editor: Dawn Stover
Senior Editor: Bob Sillery
Managing Editor: Jill C. Shomer

21ST CENTURY SOLDIER was prepared by
Bishop Books, Inc.
611 Broadway
New York, NY 10012

Editorial Director: Morin Bishop
   Project Editor: John Bolster
   Designers: Barbara Chilenskas, Vincent Mejia, Miki Sakai
   Managing Editor: Theresa M. Deal
   Assistant Project Editor: Ward Calhoun
   Photography Editor: John S. Blackmar
   Researchers: Kate Brash, Jeff Labrecque
   Copy Editor: A. Lee Fjordbotten

We welcome your comments and suggestions about *Popular Science* Books. Please write to us at:
Popular Science Books
Attention: Book Editors
PO Box 11016
Des Moines, IA 50336-1016

If you would like to order any of our hardcover Collector's Edition books, please call us at 1-800-327-6388. (Monday through Friday, 7:00 a.m.— 8:00 p.m. or Saturday, 7:00 a.m.— 6:00 p.m. Central Time).

CONTENTS

INTRODUCTION

ALMOST EVERY BEND IN THE ROAD of military history contains a new technological development paired with an innovative tactical approach. Applied together on the battlefield, these new elements yielded great leaps forward in military effectiveness.

Whether it was the invention of the stirrup, which led to armored cavalries, or the appearance of long-bow archers, who made the cavalries obsolete, transforming marriages of technology and tactics have punctuated military history from time immemorial. In World War II, Germany developed agile, lightweight tanks and deployed them in separate units, supported by aircraft, to overrun most of Europe in a new form of

OPERATION ENDURING FREEDOM

A convoy of nearly 40 light armored vehicles and Humvees prepared to depart their staging area en route to Kandahar, Afghanistan, on December 13, 2001; the battle against terrorism in the Middle East represented yet another critical turning point in the long history of American warfare.

lightning warfare dubbed blitzkrieg. The development of the nuclear ballistic missile helped shape the Cold War, in which the world's two superpowers faced off across a gulf of mutually assured destruction.

As the 21st century gets under way, another one of these historical bends in the road is before us. The horrifying terrorist attacks on New York City and Washington, D.C., in September 2001, demonstrated starkly that the United States faces an array of unpredictable new threats. In short, warfare has changed once again. The U.S.-led fight in Afghanistan differed from both the Vietnam War and the Persian Gulf War—it featured significantly more special ops troops on pinpoint missions, to name one difference—and the ongoing campaign against terrorism will probably differ even more markedly. The key to this new era of combat, as in all previous ones, is technology. The terrorists of September 11 used America's technology against it, and the United States will rely on emerging technologies—highly sensitive detection equipment, networked communications, state-of-the-art targeting systems, and robotics—to deal with threats in the future. The new combat doctrine for the U.S. military calls for lighter, faster, and more agile forces with greater access to intelligence.

The military has already taken steps toward its goal of a quicker, more flexible military, and in *21st Century Soldier* we will not only outline those steps for you, we'll also look at the history of combat technology and at its burgeoning future. To that end, we've divided the chapters in our book—each of which deals with a specific military element—into three sections. Thus, in the Aircraft chapter that begins the book, there is a section on Workhorse aircraft, one on Ready-for-Duty aircraft, and another on Cutting-Edge aircraft.

As their names imply, these categories deal with planes that are time-tested mainstays of the Air Force arsenal (Workhorses); state-of-the-art aircraft awaiting—or fresh from—their combat debuts (Ready for Duty); and experimental aircraft that could be one or two years—or one or two decades—away from deployment (Cutting Edge). In the Aircraft Workhorses section, you can read about planes like the mammoth B-52 bomber, which has been a part of the U.S. arsenal since 1952 and will remain in service well into the 21st century. Our Ready-for-Duty Aircraft section spotlights such state-of-the-art planes as the F-117 Nighthawk stealth fighter and the fearsome, ultramodern F-22 Raptor. In the Cutting-Edge Aircraft section, we look ahead to the Joint Strike Fighter, which is on the verge of deployment, and even further ahead to unmanned combat aerial vehicles and laser-equipped spaceplanes.

In our Weaponry and Gear chapters, you can read about such fabled items as the M-16 rifle and the C-Ration meal, and you can find out what the U.S. military envisions for its troops in the year 2025. In Tactics, we look back to the jungle theaters of Vietnam and the desert combat of the Persian Gulf before examining the ongoing campaign in Afghanistan and looking ahead to future scenarios. Our Armor chapter looks at Workhorses like the Humvee, which replaced the Jeep in the 1980s and will probably enjoy as long a run in the military as its predecessor did, and Ready-for- Duty equipment like the Stryker family of armored vehicles, which represent the first phase in the Army's effort to completely over-haul its armored divisions by the middle of the 21st century.

As we've said, each chapter unfolds along the same lines. We believe this structure affords the best means of assessing the military's past, present, and future—with an emphasis on the latter two. But one thing we wish to make clear at the outset is that the categories are by no means rigid: A variety of factors—most notably the status of emerging technologies—conspires to blur the lines between our definitions in some places. As a result, you may find, for example, that some of the Ready-for-Duty elements will not actually see duty for several years, or that the Cutting-Edge materials are strictly experimental at the moment—closer to science fiction than military fact. That's simply a function of the available material occasionally not fitting neatly into our categories: In our Ships chapter, for instance, we explain that the U.S. Navy has no plans to replace the aircraft carrier as the centerpiece of its fleet. Cutting-Edge ships, therefore, consist mainly of smaller support craft and high-tech additions to current members of the fleet.

But enough preliminaries—we invite you to turn the page and delve into the fascinating world of the current and future U.S. soldier. He has an astonishing array of tools at his disposal as he faces the complex challenges of the young century.

AIRCRAFT

AIRCRAFT

For a handful of years after the Wright brothers' invention of the airplane, gentlemen-designers the world over built small, speedy biplanes that could hold only the pilot, and larger, slower, two-seaters that could carry cargo. When World War I erupted during the next decade, the larger airplanes were deployed to photograph the front lines or hand-drop bombs there, while the smaller airplanes flew up to shoot larger enemy planes down. Thus aerial warfare was born.

As time passed, the warplanes' roles remained essentially the same, but technology kept advancing. Aluminum replaced the wood-and-canvas construction of warbirds, and the added strength of the metal allowed aircraft to evolve from biplanes to monoplanes. The machines gained speed in the bargain. By the time of World War II, warbirds could be thrown together from scratch in just a few months; the P-51 Mustang—perhaps the greatest U.S.-made fighter of World War II—was designed and built in fewer than 120 days. But even the fastest aircraft were limited by their piston engines and propellers to less than 500 mph, and their range was limited by the amount of fuel they could carry. And of course, all the bombs these planes delivered were "dumb," the positioning of the aircraft and gravity their only guide. To be effective, air forces had to be massive armadas.

The emergence of the aircraft carrier during World War II increased the range and potency of aircraft by providing militaries with a mobile base of operations to launch an aerial attack from almost anywhere in the world. In the final days of that conflict, both the Allied and Axis powers began working on jet-propelled aircraft. The swept-wing German Me-262 was the fastest. Using captured Me-262s as their model, the Americans developed even faster jets, such as the F-86, which achieved a 10-to-1 jet-to-jet victory ratio over their adversaries in Soviet-built MiGs in the Korean War.

The next leap forward came in 1953 with Russia's introduction of the MiG 19, the first supersonic fighter. The extra speed came from "afterburners," which sprayed jet fuel directly into the engines' exhaust. The process consumed prodigious amounts of fuel, so when the U.S. developed its first afterburning fighters, it made sure they could be refueled in midair by tankers. Bombers eventually came equipped with jet engines as well.

Adjustments were made to increase the efficiency of carriers, and versatile new jets, such as the F-14 Tomcat, which appeared in 1970, emphasized speed and lethality. By the 1990s, warplanes were faster, more powerful, and more agile than the Wright brothers could have imagined, but they were still visible to enemy ground forces using radar. To clear this last hurdle, the U.S. began building special "stealth" aircraft that absorbed or deflected radar and were thus undetectable to enemy sensors. Stealth aircraft such as the F-117 Nighthawk fighter or the B-2 Spirit bomber could knock out radar installations during a first-wave attack, clearing the way for other planes with significant radar signatures to finish the job.

The stealth warplanes' boxy shape, though, prevented them from reaching supersonic speeds. The latest aircraft to see production, the F-22, is so cunningly built that not only can it attain supersonic speeds without afterburners (so-called "supercruising"), but it also has stealth characteristics.

In the not-too-distant future, three arms of the U.S. military will share an aircraft, the F-35, or

F-16
FIGHTING FALCON

A far cry from Kitty Hawk, the sleek and stylish F-16 is a versatile, dependable mainstay of air forces the world over.

Joint Strike Fighter. One version will operate from conventional airstrips and another from carriers, while yet another will take off and land vertically to support special forces on the ground. All three versions of the F-35 will possess supercruise capability, and all will fly with stealth.

And in a development that looks back to the airplane's earliest roots—back to the years before the Wright brothers, when the only planes in the sky had no pilots—Boeing has introduced the X-45. It's an unmanned attack aircraft that will swarm enemy territory and targets, pounding missile and troop installations for a fraction of the cost of the F-35. For the attackers, of course, there will be no human cost at all, since the X-45s will be pilotless. The Pentagon expects that by 2020 one-third of all its warplanes will be uncrewed.

If only the Wrights could see their invention now.

WORKHORSES

DURABLE AND DEPENDABLE, IF NOT ALWAYS PLEASING TO THE EYE, WORKHORSE AIRCRAFT ARE THE MILITARY'S MAINSTAYS, COMBINING GRIT WITH A SURPRISING ABILITY TO ADAPT TO CHANGING TIMES.

WORKHORSES AIN'T PRETTY. They've all seen better days, and compared with what the U.S. military is currently capable of, technologically, they're pretty much plodding beasts. Though a few workhorse aircraft were designed with one role in mind, time and changing circumstances have loaded them down with different jobs. For roughly the last 25 years, their role has been to fly into our brushfire wars (and into conflicts like the one with Saddam Hussein in the Persian Gulf) before and after the enemy had been doused by the firepower of the more modern McDonnell Douglas F-15, Lockheed Martin F-16, or Lockheed F-117.

Against nations with no air force at all, or one equipped with ancient

B-52 / A-10

With 50 years of service, the B-52 Stratofortress (above) is the oldest workhorse, while the rugged A-10 Thunderbolt (opposite), appropriately nicknamed the Warthog, is the most unsightly.

AH-1 COBRA

Bristling with machine guns, rockets, and missiles, the Cobra—which first saw duty in Vietnam and remains in service today—was the first helicopter designed to carry arms into combat.

MiG-21s and Hinds donated years ago by the former Soviet Union, most of the U.S. workhorses remain pretty effective. Equipped with new smart bombs, the grizzled workhorses can usually dispatch these enemy machines and their facilities before the sun has set on Day 1 of any war.

Of the workhorses, none is more enduring—or more surprisingly so—than the Boeing B-52 Stratofortress, also known by its affectionate service nickname of "BUFF" (an acronym for "Big Ugly Fat F-----"). The B-52 is 50 years old, and Air Force analysts predict it will be in service for another 50 years. Originally designed as the Strategic Air Command's thermonuclear

bomber, the Stratofortress flew continuous patrols during the height of the Cold War. It held a crew of six and could reach any target in the world in 18 hours. A mammoth warbird, the B-52's 185-foot wing droops while the plane rests on the ground; in the air the Stratofortress's eight jet engines propel it to subsonic speeds of up to 660 mph at 20,000 feet. It can fly as high as 55,000 feet, which put it out of the range of anything but the luckiest Soviet surface-to-air missile during its Cold War patrols.

Of the 744 B-52s manufactured in the initial production run, many were converted to conventional bombers during the Vietnam War, in which BUFFs carpet-bombed North Vietnam. After that conflict, most observers expected the Stratofortress to be retired and replaced by the supersonic B-1 Lancer and the stealthy B-2 Spirit. But after engineers equipped the B-52 with cruise missiles, the ultimate workhorse air-

Spotlight   F-14 TOMCAT

The Grumman F-14 Tomcat (above) may be most famous for being the fighter plane that Tom (Maverick) Cruise flew in *Top Gun*. But there's much more than Hollywood flash to the F-14, one of the military's most prized workhorses. The all-weather jet, which first took to the skies in 1970, has a swing-wing design that enables it to catapult from a carrier at low speed, then rocket toward its target at 1,544 mph. Its crew includes a pilot and a radar- and weapons-system operator. This operator must hang on for dear life while keeping his attention glued to—among other elements—a high-magnification TV screen for identifying long-range targets. With its load of Phoenix missiles (each of which comes with its own radar system, a 90-mile range, and a $2-million price tag) the Tomcat can engage up to six different targets flying at different altitudes and speeds. It takes three F/A-18 Hornets to do the same job. And the F-14 can take out those targets before they reach deadly range.

In its attack mode, the Tomcat can not only destroy other fighters, but it can also wipe out cruise missiles and fly tactical reconnaissance missions. In the U.S.-led war in Afghanistan against the Taliban and Al Qaeda, though, the F-14 functioned as a fighter-bomber, firing smart bombs on enemy forces and their cave hideouts.

The Tomcat does have a couple of drawbacks. One is its relatively short range: 378 miles on internal fuel, and 750 miles with two 130-gallon external tanks. It's also roughly the size of a tennis court, which makes its radar signature less than stealthy. But, ideally, this Tomcat prowls after the enemy's radar has been disabled.

craft found yet another role. The B-52 could deliver cruise missiles effectively at a safe distance from an enemy country. Squadrons of the planes did just that during the Persian Gulf War, flying from Barksdale, Louisiana, to Saudi Arabia to release cruise missiles over Iraq. Later, after opposition forces had been destroyed, the B-52 dropped cluster bombs on targets in Iraq. And most recently, the B-52 could be seen circling above the mountains of Afghanistan, delivering payloads during the Bush Administration's war on terrorism.

As we've said, reliability and consistency come before beauty where workhorse aircraft are concerned. Nowhere is that more evident than in the case of the Fairchild A-10 Thunderbolt II, without a doubt the ugliest airplane ever to fly in combat. The Thunderbolt's crews refer to the plane as the Warthog, which should give you some idea of its aesthetic qualities. The plane is not only homely, it also looks as though it couldn't fly or fight a lick. With a straight-wing design, the Warthog's top speed is a *sub-subsonic* 422 mph; its twin tail and two rear-mounted engines give it a healthy radar signature; and without radar of its own, the Thunderbolt—ill-fitting name aside—can only fly in clear weather. As a final blemish, the bottoms of the Warthog's tires show when the plane flies overhead.

But pilots love the Warthog, mainly because the plane has proved practically invincible against tanks and enemy ground personnel in every American war since Vietnam. The hardy A-10 has proved its mettle in Desert Storm, Bosnia, Kosovo, and Afghanistan, and this Warthog has teeth: It's equipped with a seven-barrel, electrically driven Gatling gun that can fire 1,350 rounds of depleted-uranium shells the size of wine bottles (and weighing 1.5 pounds each). Every half-second burst expends 30 rounds of ammunition—enough to pierce the armor of an enemy vehicle from a distance of 2 miles. And the shells are incendiaries that burst into flames after penetrating that armor.

The A-10 can also take almost as good as it gives. The pilot sits inside a titanium bathtub that resists enemy ground fire. The entire aircraft is armored and can withstand blasts from 23-millimeter shells. The Warthog's twin tails enable it to fly

In Action

AH-1 COBRA

With its air-to-surface missiles, three-barrel rotary cannon, and multiple rocket launchers, the Bell AH-1 Cobra is a fearsome war machine indeed. The original helicopter gunship, the Cobra made its combat debut in Vietnam, but it was in Operation Desert Storm that the AH-1 hit its stride as a lethal instrument of warfare.

Flown by both the Army and the Marines, Cobras logged more than 18,000 hours in the Persian Gulf War. The Marines' AH-1W Super Cobra was credited with destroying more than 100 Iraqi armored personnel carriers and other vehicles, close to 100 tanks, 16 bunkers, and two air-defense sites. And like its namesake, the Cobra struck and withdrew unscathed: not a single AH-1 was lost, and none of her crews suffered so much as a scratch.

Realizing its potential along with the Cobra in Operation Desert Storm was part of the gunship's arsenal, the Hellfire missile. Previously cast as a tank-killer, the Hellfire demonstrated impressive and unexpected range in the Gulf, obliterating an entire spectrum of targets, including anti-aircraft installations, oil rigs, bridges, buildings, radar stations, and command-control centers.

even if one fin gets shot completely away, and the plane's twin engines mean it can continue to fly with one engine destroyed. The Thunderbolt can stay airborne with a good-size blast hole in its wing, and those unsightly exposed wheels serve their purpose too. They give the plane, and its pilot, a chance to survive a gear-up, belly landing. In short, the Warthog is as tough as its namesake, the Republic P-47 Thunderbolt, a heavy-duty fighter famous for excelling in almost every theater during World War II.

Another Vietnam-era aircraft still performing yeoman's duty today is the Bell AH-1 Cobra, a tough-as-nails helicopter. Thin but bristling with machine guns, rockets, and missiles under its stubby pylon wings, the AH-1 was the first helicopter designed to carry arms into combat. With its pilot seated in the rear and the gunner occupying the lower front seat, the Cobra, which is

A-10 THUNDERBOLT II

With its ungainly frame and protruding wheels, the Warthog, as the A-10 is affectionately nicknamed, is no looker, but it has served as a lethal, tough-as-nails workhorse for more than 30 years.

mostly deployed by the Marines, flies from aircraft carriers, sticks close to the terrain, and hits the enemy hard. Cobras currently come equipped with wire-guided missiles that the gunner can fly straight into a tank, or Hellfire missiles that can destroy a tank from miles away. For air-to-air combat against other helicopters, or even airplanes, the Cobra has Sidewinder missiles. For attacks on enemy troops or trucks, the AH-1 has seven-round rockets mounted under its wing stubs. But its structure shows its age: The Cobra has a skin of aircraft-grade aluminum instead of lighter composites.

Before Cobras, or any other aircraft, reach the scene of a battle, the Navy will often send the workhorse Grumman EA-6B Prowlers into the breach. In use since the Vietnam War, the Prowler is another homely plane that the military couldn't do without. Its role is simple: Catapulted from aircraft carriers during the earliest hours of any conflict, Prowlers fly in pairs into hostile territory to triangulate the position of the enemy's radar. Once they've located the radar installation, they jam its frequency. Under the Prowler's wing are several

AV-8 HARRIER II

A workhorse in support of Marines on the ground, the Harrier is equipped with infrared-guided missiles and specializes in air-to-surface and air-to-air missions in darkness and inclement weather.

radar-jamming pods, which can render seven frequencies utterly useless. A handful of Prowlers can black out an area the size of France. After completing their mission, Prowler pilots can call in F-117 Stealth hits on the installation; or a Prowler can fire high-speed anti-radiation missiles (HARM) to knock the enemy communications building off line for the safety of the rest of the air strike.

The Prowler is not a fast aircraft—its top speed is 650 mph—but it attacks at night and can keep a safe distance from any enemy radar transmitter. The plane also has extensive countermeasure systems: In addition to its radar-jamming system, which provides obvious protection, the EA-6B can drop aluminum chaff to fool the radar installation, and it can shoot flares to confuse heat-seeking missiles.

Finally, no discussion of the military's workhorse aircraft would be complete without mentioning the Marines' AV-8 Harrier II. The Harrier, which can take off and land vertically, flies in support of Marines fighting on the ground. Its top speed is 660 mph, but for its role the Harrier doesn't need supersonic speed. Attached to Marine units at forward bases, the Harrier can be called in at a moment's notice. During battle, it fires television- or infrared-guided missiles at enemy tanks, troops, or buildings. The Marines can call the Harrier in for precise strikes just a few dozen feet ahead of their position. The plane's one flaw is that its exhaust nozzles are almost precisely at the aircraft's center, making it particularly vulnerable to a strike by an enemy's heat-seeking missile. During the Persian Gulf War, the U.S. lost five Harriers.

But whatever their flaws, Harriers, like all of the workhorse aircraft, have stood the test of time. Of course, for that they owe as much to the training, skill, and courage of their crews as to the considerable ingenuity and sophistication of their technologies.

[AIRCRAFT]
READY FOR DUTY

FRESH OFF THE PRODUCTION LINE AND LOADED WITH STATE-OF-THE-ART TECHNOLOGY, READY-FOR-DUTY AIRCRAFT ARE THE MILITARY'S NEW STARS, KEEPING THE U.S. AT THE FOREFRONT OF COMBAT AVIATION.

F-22/F-117

While the Lockheed F-117 Nighthawk (opposite) sacrifices speed for stealth, its ultramodern cousin, the F-22 Raptor (above), possesses both qualities in abundance.

EMPHASIZING SPEED, stealth, agility, and computer-guided, "fly-by-wire" avionics, some of the military's most modern aircraft have spent years in development. But as today's pilots will attest, they've proven worth the wait.

Leading the pack is the Lockheed Martin F-16 Fighting Falcon, arguably the most beautiful airplane in service today. The first fly-by-wire aircraft, the Fighting Falcon was conceived by the Lightweight Fighter (LWF) program in 1972 and was ready for combat by 1980. A network of

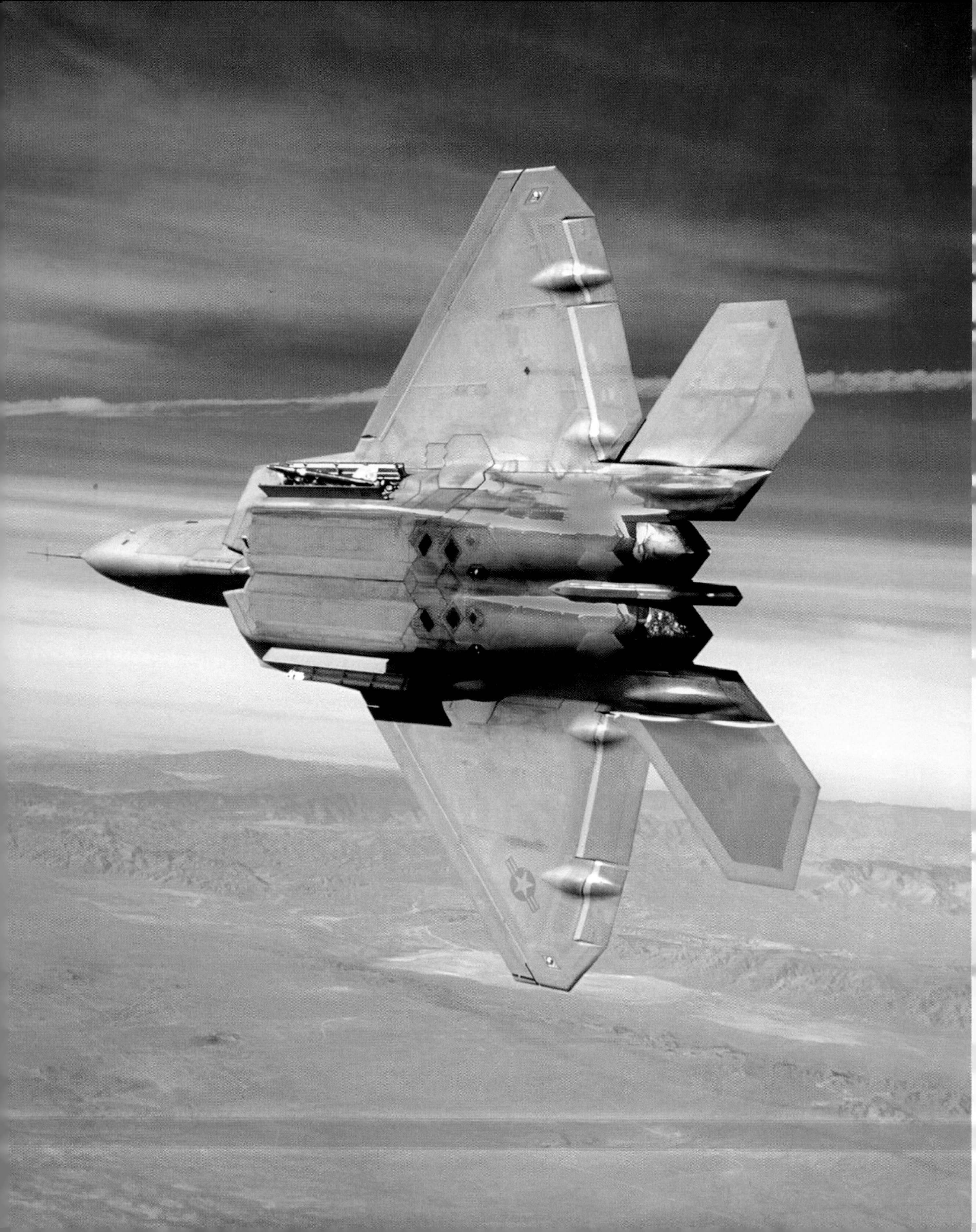

F-22 RAPTOR

Developed by Boeing, Lockheed Martin, Pratt & Whitney, and the U.S. Air Force, the Raptor is a multi-role, air-superiority fighter with an unprecedented mix of speed and stealth—and stunning agility.

computer-controlled, electronic wire bundles responds to pilot input to fly the plane, replacing the old system of cables and linkages. But this breakthrough technology was also an early source of trouble for the F-16. The wires tended to rub off their insulation against the inner framework, which caused initial versions of the aircraft to nose over and crash. (F-15 pilots nicknamed F-16s "Yard Darts.") But once engineers isolated and fixed the problem, the F-16 went on to become a favorite among fighter pilots.

In addition to making the aircraft sleeker and easier to build, the fly-by-wire controls allowed the stick to be moved from between the pilot's legs to a more comfortable position on the right side of the cockpit. The new side-mounted stick is smaller and infinitely more responsive than the previous, center-mounted version. The slightest movement of the stick to the left, right, up, or down prompts the Fighting Falcon to accomplish the corresponding maneuver. Despite this ultra-fine sensitivity, the new control system was not difficult for pilots to master.

Another design innovation in the cockpit of the Falcon is a higher seat, which gives the pilot increased visibility through the tinted bubble canopy. The seat also leans back at a 30-degree angle, which may look odd but allows the pilot to withstand higher G-forces than most other fighters, friend or foe.

While it's not the fastest plane in the U.S. arsenal, the Fighting Falcon can manage Mach 2.05 on its single Pratt & Whitney engine, with the afterburner blazing. That's nearly as fast as the French Mirage 2000 and the Russian MiG-29. The F-16 is an air-superiority fighter (with six air-to-air missiles on its wings) and also can be deployed for ground attack missions. The final winning touch for the Fighting Falcons is their price: At $14.6 million each, they're quite a bargain.

They're also fairly ubiquitous—Belgium, Denmark, Turkey, Egypt, and Israel all have them in their inventories. And if you've ever been to an airshow, chances are you've seen a Fighting Falcon in action. The U.S. Air Force Thunderbirds fly F-16s.

While the F-16 took eight years to develop, the diamond-shaped F-22 Rapier, an even more sophisticated aircraft, required nearly twice that time. In 1981 Lockheed submitted the aircraft to a competition to develop a replacement for the McDonnell Douglas F-15 Eagle. Ten years later, the F-22—renamed the Raptor—won the fly-off competition against Northrop/McDonnell Douglas's F-23.

Its name may suggest the veloceraptor dinosaur, but the F-22 is no relic; it's the most state-of-the-art aircraft in the U.S. inventory. With twin Pratt & Whitney engines, the F-22 can accelerate into "supercruise"—Air Force terminology for flying supersonic without fuel-gulping afterburners. The F-22's top speed is somewhere around Mach 2.2, or 1,500 miles per hour. (For comparison, an unencumbered F-15 can fly at Mach 2.5; an F-18 will run at Mach 1.8.)

The Raptor's engine nozzles can vector their thrust up to 20 degrees, allowing the pilot to perform stunningly tight maneuvers in dogfights. The F-22 can outrun an enemy aircraft, or, if need be, it can brake and get behind an adversary before the enemy pilot knows what's happening.

In addition to its speed and astonishing agility, the F-22 is among the stealthiest aircraft in existence. With serpentine engine inlets, a coating on the canopy that absorbs the radar return from the pilot's helmet, and its anti-aircraft missiles tucked inside the airframe, the Raptor has the radar signature of a wasp. What's more, the F-22 has a low exhaust heat to block infrared detection. Add low noise and low turbulence to these qualities, and you have an aircraft that is practically invisible to enemy detection equipment.

F-16 FIGHTING FALCON

Banking in the skies above California, a Fighting Falcon shows its fearsome talons, which include air-to-air and air-to-ground supersonic rockets. A fairly lightweight jet, the F-16 can carry 12,000 pounds of ordnance.

Like the F-16, the F-22 has fly-by-wire controls. After nearly two decades of testing and fine-tuning, the F-22 is ready for combat and is truly the fighter of the future. By the end of 2002 there will be 23 Raptors in the U.S. inventory.

They will join some 50 Lockheed F-117 Nighthawks, the so-called stealth fighters, which are equally impressive. Kept secret at the Lockheed Skunk Works in Southern California since its inception in 1978, the Nighthawk made its combat debut in December 1989, flying in Operation Just Cause, the invasion of Panama to remove General Manuel Noriega from office. The folks at Skunk Works clearly sacrificed speed for stealth: The Nighthawk flies at the decidedly subsonic speed of Mach 0.9, but the flat black surface coating its hidden engine ports and exhausts, and its angular construction, give it the radar return of a small bird.

While only two F-117s flew during the Panama invasion, the Gulf War featured many more stealth fighters: Two squadrons of Nighthawks were stationed in Saudi Arabia, and a few of the stealth fighters flew in the first raids on Baghdad. The F-117s blasted military targets with smart bombs while more traditional air-superiority fighters flew cover. And the Nighthawk did its business well: F-117s flew nearly 1,300 sorties with an 80 percent success rate and zero casualties. Every Nighthawk that flew in the conflict returned to base unscathed.

Yet for all of the stealth fighter's cutting-edge accoutrements, it has a technological Achilles heel—if all of its flight computers suddenly failed, the pilot would have to abandon ship, as the aircraft would be all but unflyable.

Joining the Nighthawk as an effective performer in the Gulf War was the McDonnell Douglas AH-64 Apache helicopter, an especially lethal machine. Walk in front of an Apache

Spotlight B-2 SPIRIT BOMBER

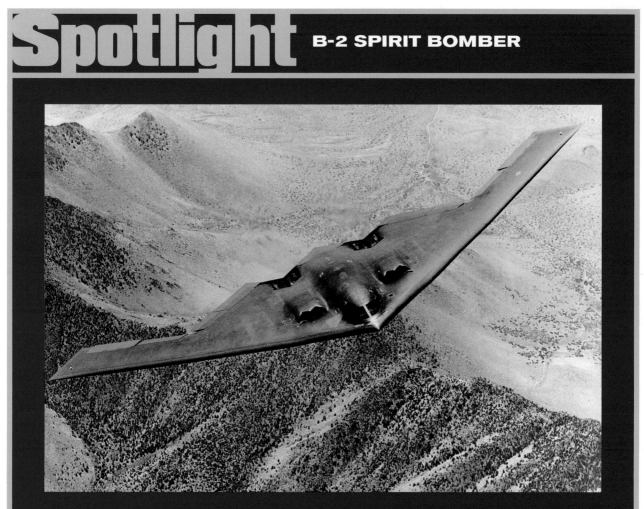

Company founder John Northrop finally got his wish: He had always wanted to sell one of his flying machines to the United States Air Force, and in 1988 he—well, his descendants—finally did. The supersecret B-2 Spirit (above) rolled out of a U.S. Air Force plant in Palmdale, California, in November 1988 for a cadre of reporters, who were allowed to photograph it only from predesignated angles lest they give away the airplane's stealthy features.

Sixty-nine feet long, 17 feet high, and with a wingspan of 172 feet, the Spirit carries two pilots and flies at a top speed of 475 miles per hour. But Air Force experts believe that the Spirit's stealth qualities can more than make up for its relatively sluggish pace. It has a 33-degree wing sweep and a trailing edge shaped like a W, which deflects enemy radar. The B-2's four GE turbofans are encased deep within the wing to prevent the fans from reflecting radar, while the exhaust is injected with chlorofluorosulphonic acid to prevent contrails from forming in the sky. The wing is coated with a black graphite-epoxy material, which absorbs radar.

All of these qualities make the Spirit, as its name suggests, something of a ghost in enemy skies. Its radar signature is roughly the size of that made by a large bird. On the downside, B-2s need care and feeding from their mechanical crews after every single sortie, and at close to $1 billion a plane, they are not cheap. The Pentagon has decided it only needs 20 of them.

While the Spirit was initially intended to function as a high-level nuclear bomber, several of them have been converted into mid-level conventional bombers, a role they filled in Afghanistan in 2001 and '02.

while the pilot sits inside, wearing his sight-mounted helmet, and marvel as he turns his head to follow you: The Apache's 30-millimeter cannon tracks you along with the pilot's eyes. On second thought, don't try that—the Apache's gun can fire 625 rounds per minute.

The praying-mantis-shaped chopper carries other deadly armaments as well. Its wing stubs haul a selection of 16 missiles or 76 folding-fin, high-explosive rockets, and its main weapon is the Hellfire, a laser-guided missile that can destroy any armored vehicle in existence and has a range of almost five miles.

The Apache is loaded with digital technology—infrared and television cameras, and a laser designation system—which, in addition to finding targets for the helicopter, can point them out for friendly ground commanders, aircraft, tanks, and soldiers. And the AH-64 is one tough bird. It can fly day or night, in any weather, and its fuselage is designed to take hits from high-explosive rounds of up to 23 millimeters. Like

AH-64 APACHE

With a 30-millimeter cannon capable of firing 625 rounds per minute, and an assortment of weapons, including the lethal, laser-guided Hellfire missile, the Apache is indeed a mean machine.

its distant cousins the F-22 and F-117, the Apache has some stealthy qualities of its own. The helicopter's twin tail rotor blades cross one another at 55 degrees to reduce noise, and its twin turboshaft engines have infrared-supressing exhaust ports to reduce the chance of being destroyed by heat-seeking missiles.

The Apache, and its Hellfire missiles, showed their chops in the Persian Gulf, devastating Iraqi tank and troop columns in advance of coalition ground soldiers. With its ultramodern technology, lethal firepower, and superior maneuverability, the Apache typifies America's ready-for-duty aircraft—all of which play a role in making the U.S. military a worthy adversary for any enemy in the world.

In Action

F-117 NIGHTHAWK STEALTH FIGHTER

Shrouded in secrecy since the production of its first prototype, code-named Have Blue, in the mid-1970s, the F-117 Nighthawk stealth fighter made its first test flight in 1977. That experimental voyage occurred—appropriately enough, given the secrecy of the project—above Groom Dry Lake Bed, Nevada, popularly known as Area 51, a place that is the subject of much speculation among UFO buffs.

Following four more years of development, the refined Nighthawk made its first flight in 1981, and production began the next year, continuing until 1990. The first F-117 unit, the 4450th Tactical Group, launched in 1983, and two Nighthawks made their combat debut in 1989, attacking the Rio

Hato barracks in Panama during the U.S.'s invasion to remove General Manuel Noriega from power.

Thirty-six Nighthawks made the trip to Saudi Arabia in 1991 to see action in U.S. Operation Desert Storm. They performed admirably, flying nightly sorties into Baghdad and destroying numerous valuable targets without suffering a single loss.

But the Nighthawk's aura of invincibility dissipated on March 27, 1999, when an F-117 was shot down by enemy fire while supporting NATO's action in the former Yugoslavia. While the pilot was rescued, the $122-million Nighthawk, and all of its stealth technology, was believed to have been captured intact.

CUTTING EDGE

AIRCRAFT OF THE FUTURE WILL RELY LESS AND LESS ON HUMAN INVOLVEMENT, EVENTUALLY RELEGATING PILOTS TO THE ROLE OF GROUNDED OPERATORS, AS COMBAT AVIATION BECOMES ENTIRELY REMOTE-CONTROLLED.

O NE DOES NOT NEED A CRYSTAL BALL, or any other instrument of prophecy, to determine that the future of combat aviation involves more planes but fewer pilots. Unmanned Aerial Vehicles (UAVs) captured both the military's and the public's imagination in 2002 after a 27-foot-long Predator drone operated by the Central Intelligence Agency fired Hellfire missiles at Taliban targets during the war in Afghanistan. Those shots, and subsequent unmanned sorties in the same conflict, proved that remote-controlled planes could handle missions that would put pilots at risk. The love affair with UAVs—which will eventually come in many shapes and sizes and perform an array of missions—had begun.

GLOBAL HAWK/ X-45 UCAV

Currently used only for recon, the unmanned Global Hawk (opposite) is poised for an expanded role; unmanned combat aerial vehicles, such as the prototype X-45s illustrated above, flying with F-16s, will soon rule the skies.

CANARD/ROTOR WING

Unmanned helicopters of the near future will be able to shift in mid-flight from rotor to wing for high-speed flight; they will be equipped with a canard rotor that will help maintain lift during the transition.

Combined with its ability to fly reconnaissance and surveillance missions for 24 hours at a stretch, the Predator's recently developed lethality opens a new chapter in military aviation—and possibly a turning point in the history of warfare. Two versions of a Predator B are waiting in the wings, one that is equipped with a turbo-prop and another that comes with a jet engine, both of which will outstrip the original's 84-mph cruising speed. Predator B will also operate at higher altitudes (up to 45,000 feet) than its predecessor, enabling it to survey vaster distances. The original $3-million Predator has a ceiling of around

25,000 feet, which sometimes made operators at home base feel like they were looking at the ground through a straw.

Another key attribute of Predator B will be a payload capacity increased from 450 pounds to 750. The new drone also will be outfitted with a Lynx synthetic aperture radar that can penetrate bad weather and is sensitive enough to spot footprints in the dirt. Predator B will be more heavily armed, perhaps carrying as many as 14 missiles, and its improved sensors should allow it to hit moving targets with greater accuracy than earlier models.

With its increased capabilities, the new Predator will probably draw more varied and more frequent assignments. If paired with its higher-flying unmanned cousin, the Global Hawk, the Predator could take over the monitoring of no-fly zones, a task currently handled

Spotlight   AIRBORNE LASER

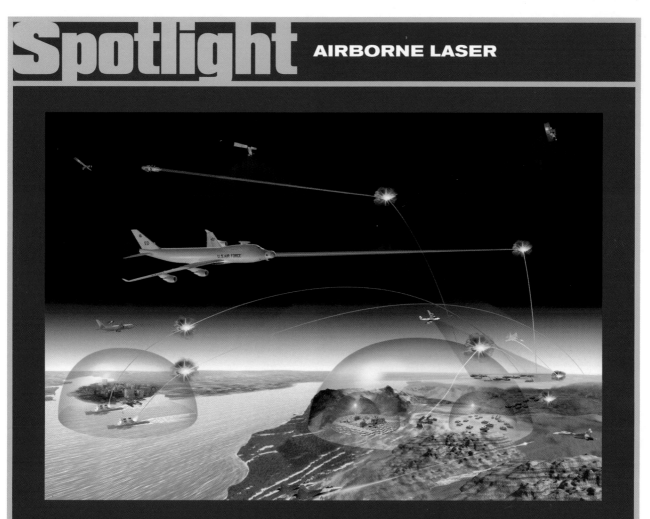

Originally envisioned in 1967 by Edward Teller, the father of the hydrogen bomb, the airborne laser (ABL) weapon is a high-flying answer to the problem of missile defense. The idea is to use a laser mounted inside a 747-400 air freighter to nip enemy missiles in the bud, shooting them down from hundreds of miles away just after they launch.

The notion didn't prove practical until the development of a chemical oxygen-iodine laser (COIL) small enough to fit on a plane. Because the laser generates its beam from a chemical reaction, large onboard electrical power sources are not required to make it work. The laser beam focuses a basketball-sized spot of heat that burns through the skin of the enemy's missile to destroy it. Advanced optics and the laser's short wavelength (1.3 microns) allow the beam to knife through any atmospheric interference and hit the target with undiminished potency. Unlike a missile, a laser can engage a target repeatedly or be directed against multiple targets in a short period of time.

ABL is being built by three companies—Boeing, TRW, and Lockheed Martin—and a prototype, the YAL-1A, is expected to fly in late 2003. The U.S. Air Force envisions a fleet of seven ABLs that could be on station anywhere in the world within 24 hours to quell a missile threat wherever it arises. Work is also under way to shrink the COIL laser to produce a "roll-on, roll-off" version that could be used on planes such as the MV-22 Osprey or on a CH-47D Chinook helicopter. These aircraft could then be used to defend against cruise missile attacks, to name one threat, in smaller battle zones. The ABL is one form of missile defense likely to arrive sooner rather than later.

X-32/X-35

The two entrants in the competition to produce a multi-service Joint Strike Fighter face off on the tarmac at Edwards Air Force Base. Lockheed Martin's sleek X-35 (right) defeated Boeing's X-32 to claim the contract.

by piloted aircraft. The jet-powered Global Hawk, with a ceiling of 65,000 feet, is being equipped with the high-powered sensors once deployed on the U-2 spyplane. Global Hawks may take over many of the U-2 missions since the drones can stay on station over a hot zone for 35 hours at a stretch, a period well beyond the endurance of any pilot. As many as 60 Global Hawks could be in service by 2010.

The Predator and its subsequent versions won't be the only UAVs packing weapons. The Army is currently testing the firing of an anti-tank munition from its short-range Hunter UAV. But the lethality planned for UAVs in the short term

pales in comparison to what the future holds. By the end of 2010, the first truly robotic warplanes should be heading into battle. The prototypes— sleek, Y-shaped aircraft that look like they came straight from George Lucas's Industrial Light and Magic company—are already being built by Boeing. Dubbed X-45s, these cutting-edge models are a prototype for robotic fighters of the future that will be able to pick their own targets and choose how best to destroy them.

Aircraft like the X-45, collectively called Unmanned Combat Aerial Vehicles (UCAVs), may eventually replace cutting-edge jets like the Joint Strike Fighter (JSF), a multi-role, multi-service warbird that is on the verge of production. Make no mistake, the versatile, supersonic JSF will be a potent addition to the U.S. arsenal, but one advantage of UCAVs is obvious: A pilot isn't at risk. Another isn't so obvious: Pitted against a piloted aircraft, a

UCAV could perform aerial maneuvers and endure G-forces that would leave the enemy pilot incapacitated. Other advantages affect the bottom line: UCAVs are a lot less expensive to build than piloted aircraft—between $10 million and $15 million per plane, or about one-third the cost of a Joint Strike Fighter. UCAVs will also cost one-third less than the Joint Strike Fighter to maintain and operate. Part of the savings will be due to a reduced personnel requirement—four or five UCAVs could be controlled by a single operator either on the ground or in a nearby plane.

At first, the X-45s will carry fairly conventional weapons, but by 2012, the UCAV's arsenal may be more exotic. It could include a high-energy laser and extremely powerful microwave weapons, both of which are in development and would be used against air-missile defenses and radar installations, executing surgical strikes that would cripple the enemy's electronics without inflicting much damage on buildings and people.

While the U.S. Air Force and Navy anticipate the arrival of ground and carrier-based UCAVs, the Army is looking for an unmanned version of its workhorse helicopters. The ability of an unmanned helicopter to land and take off vertically, as well as hover, offers obvious advantages in recon and surveillance missions. Two potential unmanned candidates, both unarmed, are being developed by the Defense Advanced Research Projects Agency (DARPA), the Pentagon's research arm, and they hint at technological breakthroughs to come. One is called the Dragonfly, an 18-foot-long craft that hovers like a chopper but moves with the speed of a jet. Its rotor blades are designed to lock into place in mid-air to become a wing, making high-speed flight possible. A forward canard and a horizontal stabilizer maintain lift during the transition from rotor to wing. A second unmanned possibility is called the Hummingbird, a 35-foot-long vehicle that would use a variable-speed rotor to conserve fuel and stay aloft for 30 to 40 hours at a time. Most current rotorcraft can stay airborne for roughly 4 hours. The Vigilante, an armed unmanned helicopter, is in the works, with a missile-firing test scheduled for late 2003.

X-45A UCAV

In September 2000, Boeing rolled out the X-45A unmanned combat aerial vehicle to meet a curious public. Twenty-nine feet long, with a wingspan of 44 feet, and weighing 10,000 pounds, the blue-and-white X-45A is tailless and possesses a distinctly sleek and futuristic-looking Y shape. Despite its compact airframe and relatively light weight, the X-45A is capable of carrying 3,000 pounds of ordnance into combat.

Boeing and the Pentagon's Defense Advanced Research Projects Agency (DARPA), which jointly developed the UCAV under a $191-million cost-share agreement with the U.S. Air Force, have pinned lofty ambitions to the X-45A's slender frame: They hope the UCAV will be able to knock out enemy air defenses and conduct precision strikes with greater accuracy than any previous aircraft—and of course, as a pilotless vehicle, with zero risk of U.S. human casualties.

The anticipated scenario for their deployment would have a squadron of X-45s setting out with preprogrammed information and preliminary targeting objectives that they could enact by themselves. Should circumstances change, however, human UCAV controllers on the ground could interact with the X-45s to adjust their action as needed.

SPACEPLANE

Riding atop its launch vehicle in this artist's rendering, the spaceplane, which would be able to monitor or attack targets the world over in minutes, represents the visible horizon of combat aviation's future.

While the combat pilot will almost surely be a historical curiosity to future warriors, his role will not be entirely eliminated, just significantly downgraded. Pilots will most likely work far from the front lines as remote-control operators of specialized aircraft. One future role may be as the remote flyer of a horde of mini-UAVs such as the Smart Warfighting Array of Reconfigurable Modules (SWARM) being developed by the U.S. Navy for deployment aboard ships in 2004. Each 4-foot-long SWARM plane costs only $2,000, so unlike larger UAVs, the mini fighters would be as expendable as the similarly priced sonar buoys the Navy readily uses and discards.

The advantage of deploying SWARMs lies in their ability to act in concert, thanks to advances in computer software governing co-operative behavior in robots. Each SWARM has a 1,500-mile range and has an Iridium satellite transceiver so it can be controlled from the other side of the world. Launched from catapults, SWARMs will have their own inexpensive sensors onboard, whether they are video or infrared cameras, or chemical or bio-hazard detectors. The collected data will be sent relay-style from one SWARM to the next toward the mother ship using undetectable, encrypted radar pulses and providing a ship's captain with an over-the-horizon view never before available.

At the other end of the pilot-of-the-future spectrum, the most coveted aviator role in years ahead may be as the pilot of the military spaceplane now in the early stages of development by NASA and the U.S. Air Force. While a prototype may not appear until 2010 at the earliest, the military spaceplane would be in position to monitor or attack targets around the globe in a matter of minutes. Unlike today's space shuttle, the military spaceplane would be able to land and relaunch

into space within as little as 24 hours. Among its potential weapons are lasers for destroying enemy space satellites, and "rods of God"—guided, uranium-enriched, hypervelocity rods that would turn hardened, underground enemy bunkers on Earth into large, empty craters.

As unmanned aircraft appear poised to eliminate the pilot's current role, he may have no choice but to enter the final frontier of space to earn his stripes.

ARMOR

ARMOR

THE WORLD'S FIRST TANKS, with their parallelogram profiles, bulky treads, and clanking gaits, appeared during World War I. Perhaps unsurprisingly, they proved incapable of breaking the stalemate of trench warfare.

Twenty years later, led by its megalomaniacal head of state, Adolf Hitler, Germany made a great leap forward in armored technology. Manufacturers had learned to use cast steel, which made tanks lighter, and to angle the tanks' armor by between 45 and 70 degrees, which deflected the enemy's weapon penetration. The result was Hitler's infamous Panzer tank divisions, agile armored vehicles that worked in concert with Stuka dive-bombers to introduce to the world a new form of warfare—Blitzkrieg, or lightning war.

With Stukas making precision strikes just 300 yards ahead of armored columns, Panzers overran Poland in 1939 and rolled through the Ardennes forest to bypass the Maginot Line and sweep over France in '40. Panzers were not only more mobile than their armored peers and predecessors, but their operators also employed more effective tactics than the French, British, Soviet, and even American armored divisions used. Whereas the Allies used tanks primarily as a screen for infantry assaults, the German line began with heavy tanks and troops and finished with lighter tanks. They used the tank as an independent weapon—an approach the Allies quickly adopted.

The German armored divisions were eventually defeated in Europe not because the Allies made technological adjustments but because the U.S.'s Sherman tanks gradually overwhelmed the German tanks by sheer force of numbers.

During the 1950s, the U.S. armed forces developed the M-48 Patton, a machine that laid the groundwork for the M-60 Patton main battle tank, which appeared in 1961. Armed with a 105mm cannon, a 7.62mm machine gun with 5,950 rounds, and a .50-caliber antiaircraft gun

with 900 rounds, the M-60 set the contemporary standard for armored vehicles. One version, the M-60A2, was so complex that its four-man crew nicknamed it Starship. The U.S. produced 15,000 M-60s, and they served in every conflict from Vietnam to the Gulf War, as well as with Israeli forces in the Yom Kippur War, in both the Sinai and the Golan Heights.

Sharing armored duty with the M-60 in the Gulf War was the M1-A1 Abrams tank. The Abrams' main armament is a 120mm smoothbore cannon, which, among other types of ammo, fires depleted uranium shells. The M1-A1 also

HUMVEE

Bigger, stronger, and tougher, the High Mobility Multipurpose Wheeled Vehicle, or Humvee, has replaced the Jeep as the military's general-purpose armored vehicle. It's also taken the Jeep's place in the hearts of U.S. soldiers.

tary's arsenal well into the 21st century. During World War II, American soldiers traveled in the M2-A1 half-track, a vehicle that traveled partly on wheels and partly on tank tread, hence its name. In Korea, U.S. infantry traveled in the M-59 and M-75—fully tracked, boxy vehicles—and in Vietnam, their armored transport vehicle was the M-113 Gavin, built during the late 1950s. The Gavin was speedy and well-liked by troops. It was recently replaced by the LAV III Stryker, a personnel carrier mounted on eight wheels, foregoing tank treads altogether. Despite its high speed—60 mph—critics say it is no match for the old Gavin. One drawback of the Stryker is its size. A C-17, the main jet transport for the Army, can hold five Gavins but only three Strykers.

The Stryker will also compete for a place in the U.S. inventory against the M2-M3 Bradley Fighting Vehicle, a tracked, heavily armed amphibious personnel carrier capable of reaching 48 mph. The Bradleys come with two machine guns and an antitank missile.

Like all armored vehicles, personnel carriers will become lighter, sturdier, and more lethal as the 21st century progresses. As for which style of armored vehicle (tracks or wheels) will win out, only time—and battle testing—will tell.

includes three machine guns, two six-barrel smoke-grenade dischargers, and six periscopes—including a thermal viewer for nighttime observations—to give the commander a 360-degree view without exposing him through the turret's porthole. And the Abrams will soon have a new gas turbine engine that allows it to run quieter, faster, and without visible exhaust. But by 2025, the Abrams, and tanks in general, will be all but obsolete. Brigades of lightweight armored vehicles with superb mobility and lethality will replace them.

While tanks' days may be numbered, armored personnel carriers will remain part of the mili-

[ARMOR]
WORKHORSES

WITH ITS RUGGEDNESS, PRACTICALITY, AND VERSATILITY, WORKHORSE ARMOR, WHICH IS ESSENTIAL TO A WIDE RANGE OF MILITARY OPERATIONS, HAS A WAY OF WINNING A SOLDIER'S DEEPEST AFFECTION.

I N THE BEGINNING, God gave the American G.I. the Jeep. And the G.I. saw that it was good.

Created during World War II as a multipurpose vehicle, the Jeep was indeed a godsend to U.S. troops. Of simple construction, it came with bucket seats up front, a bench seat in back, and room for two more soldiers over the exposed wheel wells. The Jeep's rear compartment also acted as an open trunk. The vehicle could be repaired in the field; it had huge tires with thick treads, four-wheel drive, a rugged suspension, and a 4-cylinder gasoline engine that could propel the machine to its top speed of 60 mph. The Jeep's 6-volt battery ran its electrical system, which included little more than headlights. Simple but effective, the Jeep was not

JEEP/ HUMVEE

U.S. soldiers liked the versatile and durable Jeep (opposite) so much that they found it hard to imagine an improved general-purpose vehicle– until they encountered the bigger, tougher, and even more versatile Humvee (above).

without its ingenious touches as well: The headlights could swivel inward to light nighttime repair work on the engine compartment.

American G.I.'s generated the vehicle's nickname from its official designation of G.P., or General Purpose. It may have looked boxy and ungainly, but the Jeep was fairly acrobatic. It could drive up a 40-degree slope, turn a 30-foot circle, and take mud up to its axles without getting stuck. In an emergency, one Jeep pulled 25 tons at 20 miles per hour. Its flat, olive green hood served as a card table during downtime for bored infantry and as a platform for receiving orders from officers or blessings from chaplains. With its hinged windshield lying forward, the Jeep could act as a stretcher bearer for wounded soldiers.

Rugged, durable, and tremendously utilitarian, the Jeep elicited deep affection from U.S. G.I.'s. A single frame drawn by the World War II cartoonist Bill Mauldin summed up this feeling. It pictured a Jeep damaged beyond repair and a muddy, distraught American soldier sadly preparing to put a bullet through its hood.

The Jeep served in three wars—World War II, Korea, and Vietnam—before the U.S. military decided to put it down in favor of a developing successor, the High Mobility Multipurpose Wheeled Vehicle, or HMMWV, which soldiers quickly nicknamed the Humvee.

The challenge to replace the beloved Jeep had seemed all but impossible, but several companies took it on anyway, and in 1983, AM General

M-60 PATTON TANK

After waiting almost two decades, the M-60 Patton Main Battle Tank made a successful U.S. combat debut during Operation Desert Storm; more than 20 nations keep the rugged and reliable Patton in their arsenals.

won a contract to build 55,000 Humvees. The military's current all-purpose workhorse vehicle, the Humvee manages, against all expectations, to make the Jeep look like a weak sister. Propelled by a 6.5-liter, 170-horsepower diesel engine (diesel powers most of the military's heavy vehicles), the Humvee, despite being roughly twice the size of a Jeep, can roar down the highway at 70 mph. It incorporates full-time four-wheel drive and has a Central Tire Inflation

System that allows the driver to deflate the vehicle's huge tires for extra traction.

Fully loaded, the Humvee clears the ground with 16 inches to spare, and it climbs over 18-inch-high obstacles as though they were speed bumps. The Humvee is flat and broad, and its wheelbase is wide enough to follow in the tracks of an M1-A2 Abrams tank—or most other armored vehicles, for that matter. The most recent models have 190-horsepower turbo mills instead of the 170-horse units of their predecessors.

Expanding the already considerable versatility of the Jeep, the Humvee comes in four main styles: a two-door hardtop, a four-door hardtop, an open top, and a wagon, which can carry eight troops. These four types have been factory-modified into six subtypes: the cargo-troop carrier, the armament carrier, the missile carrier, the ambulance, the shelter carrier, and the prime mover. Our apologies to Mr. Mauldin and to World War II veterans, but the Humvee has taken the Jeep's place in the hearts of U.S. soldiers.

With a towing system that can handle 4,200 pounds, the Humvee is a muscle car, but without the speed typically associated with such vehicles. Or the brakes: It requires 26 seconds to go from 0 to 50, and 176 feet to stop. For $80,000, you can experience these limitations, as well as the many impressive assets, of the Humvee, firsthand. That's how much the civilian Humvee, called the Hummer, goes for, not including options such as a diesel engine, central wheel inflation, and an inside finish, which raise the price to $110,000. But hey, who needs a Jaguar when you can have all that muscular machinery in your driveway?

But if you really want to get your neighbors' attention, try to get your hands on an M-60 Patton Main Battle Tank. The M-60's production run occurred from 1960 to 1983, but its first, and so far only, action with U.S. forces came in the Gulf War. The tank was too heavy for action in Vietnam, where it would have bogged down in the swamps. (The 48-ton M-48 Patton was a barely-adequate substitute for the M-60 in that conflict; it didn't sink in the marshland, but the

M-48's long-range, computerized fire control—designed for war with the Soviets in Europe—was ill-suited to the close-range combat in Vietnam.)

The M-60 Patton made its combat debut with the Israeli army during the 1973 Yom Kippur War. With its 105-mm main gun, its four-man crew, and its 750-horsepower V-12 multi-fuel engine powering it to a top speed of 30 mph, the M-60 performed capably. The tank also has an air filter—which thankfully hasn't been tested in battle—that protects its crew against nuclear, biological, and chemical warfare. If need be, the M-60 can use the six-barrel smoke generators on its sides to lay a smokescreen. A total of 210 Pattons led U.S. Marine forces into Kuwait during the Gulf War, and Patton tanks currently serve with the armed forces of more than 20 nations.

As admirably as the M-60 performed in Kuwait, another Main Battle Tank, the M1-A2 Abrams, was the shining star of the Gulf War. Abrams tanks destroyed almost all of the Iraqi tank fleet, and of the 2,000 Abrams deployed, all but 18 returned in working condition.

The Abrams, like most tanks, was named

Spotlight
M2-M3 FIGHTING VEHICLE

Despite weighing 70 tons, the M1-A2 Abrams Main Battle Tank is a speedy monster: Its 1,500-horsepower engine can cruise at 30 mph and reach a top speed of 42 mph. Mechanized infantry in their Vietnam-era M113 Armored Cavalry Vehicles just couldn't keep up with it, or so the Army said. This presented a significant problem: If infantry were arriving late to the battle, they couldn't support the tanks. So the Army asked for the Bradley Fighting Vehicle, also known as the M2-M3, which first appeared in 1983.

The Bradley (below) weighs 25 tons (or 35 tons with additional armor), and comes with two missile-launch tubes, a 7.62-mm machine gun, and a 25-mm cannon near the turret. (The M113 had twin M-60s, a 40-mm grenade launcher, and a single .50-caliber machine gun.) The Bradley also has six gun ports on its sides and rear from which infantrymen can fire their M-16 assault rifles. The M2-M3 carries a crew of three, and six infantry. (The M113 needed a crew of six, including two M-60 gunners and two loaders, one of whom would also carry the grenade launcher, and it held 11 troops total). The Bradley has a 500-horsepower engine and a range of 300 miles, and, like both the M113 and the Abrams Tank, it cruises between 30 and 35 mph, with a top speed of 42 miles per hour. The six soldiers exit the Bradley by lowering a door in the rear of the vehicle.

Though the Bradley's features appear roughly equal to those of the M113, the Bradley is the superior armored vehicle, according to the Army.

after a general, Creighton Abrams, U.S. Army Chief of Staff at the end of the Vietnam War. Like the Patton, the Abrams waited a long time for its combat debut. First built in 1978, it didn't see action until its star turn in the Gulf War. A 70-ton behemoth, the M1-A2 has a 1,500-horsepower multi-fuel turbine engine (it will run on almost any type of fuel) and can attain a top speed of 42 mph. The Abrams' range is 265 miles at cruise speed—approximately 30 miles per hour, and the tank can go from 0 to 20 in only 7.2 seconds.

The M1-A2 has toughness and versatility to go with its speed. Most rounds simply bounce off its depleted-uranium armor. The M1-A2's gun turret is very agile—making it the perfect platform for defending or attacking a larger number of enemy tanks. Aside from its two 7.62-mm machine guns, and another .50-caliber machine gun mounted on a powered rotary platform, it has a 120-mm cannon protruding from its turret.

But it's what's inside that really counts. The Abrams uses the Army's Command and Control software, which allows the crew to receive and transmit digital situation data. The tank features

M1-A2 ABRAMS TANK

Most rounds simply bounce off the depleted-uranium armor of the M1, which, despite weighing 70 tons, can go from 0 to 20 in 7.2 seconds and attain a top speed of 42 mph. The M1 excelled in the Gulf War.

six periscopes that provide a 360-degree view, and it's also equipped with the Commander's Independent Thermal Viewer for a magnified image of the exterior terrain during day or night. The commander also has digital color terrain maps on a flat screen, while the gunner's equipment includes a thermal imaging sight with a laser rangefinder for firing at night with increased range. The driver gets an integrated display and thermal-management system. And the tank is equipped with a two-axis GPS unit that greatly improves its firing accuracy.

Like the Patton, the Abrams can create its own smokescreen, and it has air filters for protection against chemical, biological, and nuclear attack. Lastly, the Abrams comes relatively cheap at $2.6 million. It's a classic piece of workhorse armor: tough, dependable, practical, and relatively inexpensive.

[ARMOR]
READY FOR DUTY

**THE COMBAT DEMANDS OF THE 21ST CENTURY HAVE
GENERATED A SHIFT TOWARD LIGHTER, MORE AGILE
ARMORED VEHICLES—AND SPELLED THE BEGINNING OF
THE END FOR THAT FABLED BEHEMOTH, THE TANK.**

M1-A1/M2-A1/M-113

A group of M1-A1 and M2-A1 tanks (above) participates in a mock battle during a joint exercise between the Republic of Korea and the U.S. Two U.S. soldiers (opposite) put their M-113 Armored Personnel Carrier through its paces during training in Germany.

THE CHANGING NATURE OF WAR is gradually nudging the heavy tank toward extinction. The first hint of this trend came during Saddam Hussein's invasion of Kuwait in 1990. Had Iraqi tanks moved to attack neighboring Saudi Arabia, the two U.S. Army light divisions stationed there at the start of the hostilities would not have been able to stand up to the invasion for very long. Hussein's army never attacked Saudi Arabia, and that was fortunate for the Saudis, and the world oil market, because it took the United States months to ship its heavy Abrams tanks into position to defend against the possibility.

The second sign of trouble for heavy tanks came during the 1999 war in Yugoslavia. The country's crumbling roads often couldn't support the

STRYKER VEHICLES

The Stryker family of highly mobile light armored vehicles includes an infantry carrier (above) and a mobile gun system (above, right). There are 10 variants on the Stryker platform, and the Army will deploy 2,196 of the vehicles.

70-ton weight of the Abrams tank. The Army's most powerful land weapon was too muscle-bound to get into the fight. The conclusion was inescapable: Armor's punch would have to come in a smaller package.

The U.S. Army's solution is to implement a multiyear transformation program that will produce lighter, faster armored vehicles that can be deployed quickly by air. Currently, the Army classifies six of its 10 armored divisions as "heavy," meaning they are comprised of Abrams

tanks and the 25-ton Bradley Fighting Vehicle. In the long term (see Cutting Edge), the Army plans to overhaul its armored divisions under the program called the Future Combat System (FCS). Perhaps a decade away, this program will consist of multiple divisions of advanced lightweight armored vehicles. But before the FCS becomes a reality, the Army will deploy an interim force of six brigades equipped with the new Stryker family of light armored vehicles. The first new vehicles the Army has purchased in more than a decade, the Strykers are extremely mobile on the ground and portable by air. One of them can fit onto a C-130 cargo plane, two on a C-17, and four on a C-5.

Named after two unrelated Medal of Honor winners from World War II and the Vietnam War,

the baseline Stryker—there are 10 variants of a common platform—is essentially an eight-wheeled, overgrown armored car. Each brigade will have 366 of them. They can travel up to 60 mph over a range of 310 miles before refueling.

The Stryker variants include a nine-man infantry carrier; a mobile gun system; an anti-tank vehicle equipped with guided missiles; a reconnaissance vehicle; a fire support vehicle; a mortar carrier; a commander's vehicle; a medical unit; an engineer squad vehicle; and a vehicle dedicated to sniffing out nuclear, biological, and chemical (NBC) threats. The Army will spend $4 billion to acquire 2,131 Strykers through 2008, when it will begin acquiring next-generation vehicles. While the first of the interim Stryker-equipped brigades is expected to be

combat-ready by May 2003, not all of the Stryker variants will be available by then. The mobile gun system, the fire support vehicle, and the NBC vehicle won't be ready until 2005. Until then, the Army will supplement the brigades with vehicles currently in use.

Slimming down isn't easy, however. The target weight for each fully loaded Stryker is 38,000 pounds, the maximum weight that a C-130 can transport. Some early versions of Stryker variants checked in over the limit. The mobile gun vehicle, which uses the same 105mm cannon as did the first Abrams tanks, exceeded the weight limit by 3,000 pounds. Also, the Stryker's height makes it a tight fit aboard the C-130, so it may need to make its air journeys with the tires deflated. Fortunately, the Stryker is equipped with run-flat tires.

Spotlight SMARTRUCK

The U.S. Army's National Automotive Center is currently developing a state-of-the-art truck that would make a modern-day James Bond trade in his stylish sports car. Called the SmarTruck, this concept vehicle is unimpressive at first glance—exactly the profile you want when you're operating under cover. But underneath its unassuming façade, the SmarTruck (above) is a fearsome machine.

At the push of a button, sliding doors in its roof part to reveal a laser cannon equipped with four cameras for targeting. The gunner controls this weapon, which can rotate nearly 360 degrees, with a joystick. Bulletproof glass and lightweight armor made from Kevlar cover the SmarTruck and protect the gunner and his crew. If the situation requires it, they can take more active defensive measures as they speed away from danger—all of them deployed, à la 007, using

touchscreen panels on the dashboard. These measures include a smoke screen, oil slicks, pepper spray, and a tack dispenser. Front and rear dazzlers in the headlights can blind would-be pursuers.

While blinding adversaries, the SmarTruck does the opposite for its driver, with built-in night-vision equipment. And should the bad guys get as far as the SmarTruck's door handles, they'll get an electric shock for their trouble. Even if they get inside the vehicle, they won't be able to commandeer it; the SmarTruck won't work without fingerprint authentication.

This high-tech vehicle can also foil stealthier attacks—it has bomb detectors that will register disturbances in the vehicle's magnetic field, alerting the driver with a flashing green light on the dash. Q would be pleased.

General Motors, which is manufacturing the Stryker family, may substitute lighter materials such as aluminum for heavier steel to reduce the vehicles' weight, but that reduction could come at the expense of protection. The Stryker's half-inch armor is supposed to be able to stop 7.62mm and 14.5mm armor-piercing rounds, but recent tests proved that the vehicles were vulnerable to 14.5mm heavy-machine-gun rounds. The company is currently retrofitting the first batch of 366 Strykers with high-density ceramic armor plates, and it is unclear if this addition will push the Stryker over the 38,000-pound weight limit. If so, the vehicles will have to cut some equipment and possibly some ammunition from their loads.

If the Strykers can't stick to their diets, the

HYBRID-ENGINE HUMVEE

Officers at Fort Gillem in Forest Park, Georgia, demonstrate the U.S. Army's first Humvee equippped with a hybrid electric motor. The hybrid Humvee outperforms the conventional one in acceleration and fuel economy.

Army may have to rely on an armored personnel carrier, the M-113, to make its interim brigade vision viable. The M-113, a tracked vehicle that predates the Bradley Fighting Vehicle, fits easily into a C-130, and five can fit into a C-17. Most of the 17,000 M-113s available are in storage, though, and if the Army wants to haul them out for action, it will have to convert their communications systems to digital and upgrade their tracks.

While the future looks bright for light armored vehicles and dim for tanks, the 70-ton monsters of the battlefield will not disappear altogether. Since no land vehicle announces the military's arrival with more authority than a tank, its pyschological effect in peacekeeping missions or diplomatic missions can be profound. The Abrams tank will probably remain in the U.S. arsenal for years, despite its slow speed of 42 mph.

By 2012, the Army expects to have rebuilt 1,174 Abrams tanks, replacing everything but their hulls. Among the improvements the Army plans are a better engine that provides faster acceleration, a digital communications network that provides real-time battle data on digital

color displays, and thermal sights for both the gunner and the commander so the commander can search for new targets while the gunner fires on the ones already identified. These improvements will allow the Abrams tank to operate more effectively at night and extend its operational range. The Abrams tanks of the 4th Infantry Division already have these upgrades. During exercises in April 2002, the 4th Division operated over an area of 50 kilometers, twice its normal range, thanks largely to its improved ability to move effectively at night.

The military may also be on the verge of replacing the internal combustion engines currently driving its armored vehicles with hybrid electric propulsion. United Defense, a large military contractor, installed a 500-hp hybrid engine in an M-113 Armored Personnel Carrier

The Other Side

IRAQI ARMOR

Following its eight-year war with Iran, and the heavy losses it suffered in the Persian Gulf War, Iraq has struggled, with some success, to restore its military might.

The pre-Gulf War Iraqi Army consisted of roughly 1.7 million troops and could deploy eight armored/mechanized divisions. The reconstituted Iraqi military probably has about half as many troops and five or six armored/mechanized divisions. The majority of Iraq's Main Battle Tanks are Modified T-54s or T-55s, both of which are Soviet-made and descendants of the T-34, which Russia deployed in World War II. Iraqi armored divisions also include Soviet-made T-72 tanks, G6 Self-Propelled Gun (SPG) systems, and Multiple Launched Rocket Systems (MLRS).

This armor, combined with the Iraqi military's ongoing rebuilding process, keeps Iraq among the strongest nations in the Gulf.

(APC) to demonstrate some of the benefits hybrids can offer. The vehicle can store power, recovered from its braking process, in batteries to use later for acceleration and hill climbing. PEI Electronics performed a similar demonstration, equipping a Humvee with a hybrid electric motor. The vehicle accelerated from zero to 50 mph in 7 seconds; a standard Humvee takes 14 seconds to do the same. The hybrid Humvee also climbed a 60-degree grade at 17 mph; a regular Humvee can do it at 7 mph. And the electric motor doubled the Humvee's fuel economy to 16 miles per gallon.

Electric propulsion systems will be critical also to the development of an emerging class of weapons for armored vehicles. Electromagnetic guns, or rail guns, could be powered by the recovered energy stored in the batteries of electric armored vehicles. Rail guns use high-current pulses to fire projectiles at hypervelocities of up to 5 kilometers per second, with a range well beyond that of conventional weapons. Various departments in the armed forces and several contractors are working on ways to control the current pulses to prevent damage to the projectile during its high-speed launch. And the military is already testing

launchers ranging in bore size from 15- to 90mm, and from 1 to 10 meters in length.

Armored vehicles may also soon come equipped with a 120mm gun that uses electrothermal-chemical (ETC) propulsion to fire a dart-like projectile at hypervelocity speeds of more than 2 kilometers per second. A 120mm ETC gun would hit a target with the force of a conventional 140mm projectile. Both the ETC and the rail gun can stop enemy tanks equipped with explosive reactive armor designed to deflect or diffuse the impact of incoming rounds. Lastly, if the designers can make the systems small

M-113 APC

U.S. troops man an M-113 Armored Personnel Carrier on patrol outside of Check Point 65 in Kosovo on August 8, 2000. The M-113, which has several variants, may soon be equipped with a hybrid electric engine.

enough, high-powered lasers may eventually appear on armored vehicles.

The same electric batteries that power these new weapons will also power electromagnetic armor that will actively repel munitions, helping to ensure the vehicles' crews will be around to fight another day.

CUTTING EDGE

WITH AN EYE TOWARD SPEED OF DEPLOYMENT AS WELL AS SPEED ON THE BATTLEFIELD, THE U.S. MILITARY PLANS TO COMPLETELY TRANSFORM ITS ARMORED DIVISIONS BY THE MIDDLE OF THE 21ST CENTURY.

TANKS ARE HISTORY. Forget about those lumbering, tracked behemoths that dominated 20th century land warfare. What good are these slow giants if they take months to deploy? By the time heavy, main battle tanks arrive on the scene of a mid-21st century conflict, the fight will be long over. And if they should arrive while a battle still rages, their slow movement would make them easy targets for sophisticated anti-tank weapons and guided missiles, particularly those that attack from above, as armor is thinnest on top.

The need for speed is already a part of military doctrine. The U.S. Army wants to be able to deploy a combat-ready brigade anywhere in the world within 96 hours, a full division in 120 hours, and five divisions within 30

HUMVEE/ FCS

A U.S. soldier (above) consults his Humvee's rugged, shock-mounted computer during a "digital battlefield" experiment, which features networked communication similar to that in a Future Combat System scenario (opposite, in artist's rendering).

FCS CLOSE-COMBAT VEHICLE

The Future Combat System will include 16 to 20 armored vehicles based on a common platform. Equipped with highly sensitive detection and targeting technology, the potent close-combat vehicle will take the place of the tank in a variety of situations.

FCS CLOSE-COMBAT VEHICLE

The close-combat vehicle concept, as this artist's cross-section illustrates, employs a two-man crew, rocket launchers, and a 40mm auto cannon. All FCS vehicles will share the same frame, chassis, and drive train, and none of them will weigh more than 16 tons.

days. Seventy-ton tanks can't make the grade, but lighter, stronger, faster armored vehicles can. These new wheeled armored vehicles will weigh no more than 16 tons each for easy air transportation and come equipped with robotic drones capable of operating on the ground or in the air.

The key to survivability, though, is armor. In the past, tank manufacturers added protection, in the form of heavy steel plates, at the expense of speed. Armored vehicles in the future will use dual-layer, "smart," or reactive, armor that uses

sensors to detect an incoming round. The sensors will be part of a package that includes an explosive charge sandwiched between the two layers of armor. Just before an incoming round hits the tank, the charge will explode, blowing off an outer plate of armor but, more important, releasing energy against the incoming round. This energy deflects, disperses, or destroys the incoming projectile, minimizing damage to the tank. Army researchers estimate that this type of proactive protection is 20 times more effective

FCS NLOS 155

As lightweight and mobile as its cousins in the Future Combat System, the Non-Line-of-Sight 155mm cannon vehicle will be the most potent of the FCS's heavy artillery, capable of firing guided, or "smart," munitions at targets up to 40 kilometers away. The NLOS will have a crew of three, including the gunner.

FCS RESUPPLY VEHICLE

A general-purpose vehicle with substantial freight capacity and a crew of two (driver and commander), the FCS resupply vehicle will be equipped with embedded semiautonomy, which will allow it to operate as an unmanned follower.

than steel. To make its tanks lighter, the military will shift to armor plates made from tough ceramic or composite materials.

Galvanized by this conceptual leap forward, DARPA, the Pentagon's research arm, is working with Boeing and Science Applications International Corp. to develop the next generation of armored vehicles, which should be ready for duty by 2012. Called the Future Combat System (FCS) program, the plan calls for the development of a family of 16 to 20 vehicles built on a shared platform. The chassis and other basic features will be identical in all of the vehicles. All of them will use hybrid electric-drive propulsion systems and fuel cells that will propel the vehicles to speeds of up to 60 mph with good fuel economy. The suspension system may be variable, meaning the vehicle could increase its ground clearance to surmount obstacles or reduce it to hunker down for protection. The program's modular, common approach means that all of the vehicles will fit on C-130 transport planes.

SCAN EAGLE UAV

Unmanned aerial vehicles (UAVs) such as the Scan Eagle will be crucial to the U.S. military's Future Combat System (FCS): Each FCS unit will carry pods of UAVs equipped with state-of-the-art surveillance technology.

Almost as important as protection for these new lightweight vehicles is firepower, and the FCS vehicles will include both line-of-sight and long-range weapons. The most advanced of them will be some type of laser or high-powered microwave weapon. More traditional weapons will include a 105- to 120mm cannon with a range of 15 kilometers; a 120- to 155mm cannon with a range of 40 kilometers using "smart," guided munitions; a 120mm mortar; and a 25- to 50mm auto cannon capable of firing both standard and airburst rounds.

For use in peacekeeping missions, these armored vehicles will come equipped with a variety of nonlethal weapons ranging from stingballs to malicious aerosols to sticky foam. They might also have a heatray, mounted on top of the vehicle, that delivers a temporary burning sensation to the skin; or an acoustic blaster that penetrates any hearing protection.

GPS receivers will help the FCS vehicles put shells on target. The new vehicles also will have fire-control systems that should improve accuracy by as much as 30 percent for stationary firing and as much as 500 percent for firing while on the move. The eyes of an FCS convoy will be the reconnaissance, surveillance, and target acquisition (RSTA) vehicle, recognizable by its tall mast. The RSTA's onboard sensors include thermal imagers, TV cameras, laser rangefinders, and ground-penetrating radar. The RSTA will use other electronic systems to detect obstacles and biological or chemical hazards. Enhanced imaging software and improved identification methods

Spotlight NET FIRE

One way to get increased firepower into a battle zone quickly is to bring in boxes of missiles. That's the concept behind a DARPA program called Net Fire. It could be more accurately named Rockets in a Box.

Net Fire launchers can be mounted on a Humvee, an armored personnel carrier (right, in concept illustration), or almost any other platform at hand. Each Net Fire is a box with 16 sections—15 that hold missiles and one dedicated to command-and-control functions.

Each box has its own power system and can fire two types of vertically launched missiles. One is a guided missile designed to deliver a big bang as soon as possible—it flies fast and carries a highly explosive warhead. The other type of missile will deploy small wings after launching so it can loiter over a combat area and wait for targeting instructions. Forward troops or umanned aerial drones will deliver these instructions. The missile's loitering time will be about 30 minutes, and it will have a range of 70 kilometers. Net Fire will be an alternative to traditional artillery pieces, outstripping them in speed of deployment.

will help the four-man RSTA crew see during the chaos of combat. And should there be any doubt about the safety of the road ahead during combat, a 1-ton unmanned ground vehicle (UGV) will be sent to reconnoiter. Called the Mule, this unmanned vehicle will carry most of the sensing equipment of an RSTA and can move fast enough to accompany ground troops.

The FCS program includes 10-man armored personnel carriers as well as command, communications, medical, and automated resupply vehicles. Perhaps the most unusual vehicles in the family, however, are a launcher/carrier for small unmanned aerial vehicles (UAVs), and a separate command vehicle to control them. The launcher/carrier will carry a pod of 32 small UAVs and a two-man crew (a driver and a commander). The control vehicle will have four workstations for UAVs, and UGVs like the Mule, and accommodate a driver and a commander as well.

One UAV proposed for the Future Combat System will carry a 75-pound payload of sensors that includes TV cameras, advanced radar, target designators, multi-spectral imagers, and GPS receivers. The 300-pound UAVs, which will be tube- or rail-launched, will also possess a secure two-way communications system linked to computer networks. They will be capable of flying to an altitude of 1,500 feet, with a range of up to 30 kilometers and 10 hours of flight time. Their power will come from high-density diesel engines, fuel cells, or electric propulsion.

As the military continues its general shift toward unmanned technology, individual soldiers of the 21st century will have their own UGVs capable of performing reconnaissance missions. These mini UGVs will have a mast-mounted sensor suite that will transmit images and will work both day and night. They will also be highly maneuverable, capable of climbing stairs and able to negotiate doorways and rubble-strewn urban combat zones.

All of this equipment may foreshadow an entirely robotic class of armored vehicles that will take over specialized, hazardous tasks like mine clearing and reconnaissance and eliminate the risks involved. Robotic recon vehicles contributed to the effort at the World Trade Center in New York City following the terrorist attacks there. Equipped with tiny video cameras, these machines squeezed into spaces too narrow for humans to search for survivors or their remains. This technology will only improve, as numerous companies are currently working on a variety of military robots.

One of the most interesting of these concepts in development borrows its design from marsupials. Dubbed Raptor, this bot would be air-dropped into hostile territory, where it would release a team of smaller "munitions bots" or M-bots. They would scout the area and wirelessly relay their collected data back to the mother bot for transmission to a command post. A larger UGV called the PackBot is in the works at iRobot, a company in Massachusetts. PackBot looks like a miniature tank without a gun turret, and it's equipped with a computer, video cameras, wireless transceiver, GPS receiver, and digital compass. Its missions include transporting ammo and working as a mobile first-aid station; the PackBot can even drag a stretcher behind it for

ROBART III

While Terminator-like robotic warriors remain firmly in the province of science fiction, the U.S. Navy's Robart III, which fires a multi-barrel Gatling gun, draws mechanized warriors one step closer to reality. A remote-control operator maneuvers the Robart III, which is incapable of autonomous decision-making.

PACKBOT

Currently in development for the U.S. military, the Packbot has a computer, video cameras, and GPS technology. It will transport supplies and function as a mobile first-aid station.

a wounded soldier to roll onto and catch a ride to safety.

But how far are we from the development of Terminator-like robotic fighting machines made from practically indestructible materials? Such a development would bring new meaning to the term "armored personnel." The U.S. Navy's Robart III may be a progenitor to a fighting robot. It carries a multi-barrel Gatling gun, but currently fires only nonlethal darts. And it has operational hurdles to clear. Robart III doesn't operate autonomously—a remote-control technician operates it—and it has no ability to make autonomous decisions. The computer software that mimics the human brain's decision-making process remains the province of science fiction, for now. Any Terminator-style robot would need to be able to evaluate incoming data (Is that gunfire, fireworks, or a car backfiring?) and determine an appropiate response (Do nothing, flee, fight.). The number of sensors and microprocessors, and the layered analysis, required of them for such an evaluation—to say nothing of the power-supply logistics—is enough to ensure that robots will not entirely replace humans in combat anytime soon.

The Other Side

CHINA'S TYPE 98 TANK

A 50-ton machine powered by a 1,500-hp engine, China's latest tank, the Type 98, represents a substantial leap forward in that nation's tank technology. Also known as the WZ-123, the Type 98 features a new, boxy turret, and apparently borrows many of its features from Soviet/Russian tank designs. The Type 98's armor, for instance, appears to be based on that of the Russian T-80U tank, and the 98's 125mm main gun, along with its carousel autoloader, are believed to have Soviet/Russian origins.

But the Type 98's most significant feature was developed in China, and it appears to be unique. It's a self-defense weapon that uses a high-powered laser against enemy weapons optics and gunners.

It may be a prototype, but the Type 98 provides a glimpse of the future of China's tank technology.

SHIPS

SHIPS

AVAL HISTORY REACHED A TURNING point on August 12, 2000, when the pride of Russia's Northern Fleet, the *Oscar II*-class submarine *Kursk*, sank during training exercises in the Barents Sea off Norway. The catastrophe—probably caused by an onboard torpedo misfire—was not only a terrible disaster in which all hands (118) were lost, it also confirmed publicly what U.S. Navy strategists had recently begun to suspect privately: The Russian Navy was no longer capable of extending its power into the world's oceans—and neither was any other potential U.S. adversary. Significant threats to the U.S. Navy's ships at sea had essentially vanished. With this realization, U.S. Navy doctrine shifted in focus from "deep blue" operations to "brown water" efforts working the littoral, or coastal, regions of the world in support of land operations.

The shift meant the closing of the Cold War chapter of naval combat, which had prevailed for the previous half century. If any naval action typified the Cold War scenario, it was the cat-and-mouse game played between Soviet and American submarines in the world's oceans. That game sometimes got very dangerous indeed. Each side's fast-attack subs would attempt to track the others' "boomers," massive submarines carrying nuclear payloads that were literally apocalyptic in power. It's not difficult to imagine how this situation ocasionally veered into frightening territory.

As the 21st century begins, Russia, heir to the Soviet Union's nuclear capabilities, and the United States are preparing to reduce their nuclear weapons stockpiles. So too will the U.S. Navy reduce its number of Trident or *Ohio*-class boomers. By 2004, it will convert the four oldest vessels in the Trident fleet to conventional guided-missile submarines. In their new role, these Tridents will host contingents of special operations forces, ready to surreptitiously enter enemy waters.

The other significant ship of the latter half of the 20th century, the aircraft carrier, will continue to play a vital role in the 21st century. The carrier replaced the battleship as the star of the fleet after Pearl Harbor, and the recent conflicts in the Persian Gulf and Afghanistan demonstrated the carrier's continued importance. The ability to quickly dominate an enemy's airspace remains paramount, and since potential land bases for aircraft can always be denied for one political reason or another, the aircraft carrier is the only reliable base of operations for air missions. Many of the U.S. air strikes against Afghanistan originated from carriers.

While submarines and aircraft carriers will continue to fill important roles in the 21st century,

admirals in the coming years will sometimes direct battles from an *Arleigh Burke*-class destroyer. With their computer-controlled radar systems, these workhorse ships are assuming a new role. They can now be linked together to form a network that provides commanders with both an over-the-horizon view to sea, and a look back inland, enabling the destroyers to double as the communications hub for the fleet. Completing the destroyers' transformation from ships that assumed deep-sea–oriented duties, such as anti-submarine warfare, to vessels crucially involved in land attack, is the addition of a new, state-of-the-art 5-inch gun. The new weapon will employ Global Positioning System (GPS) technol-

USS *CURTIS WILBUR*

Outfitted with new sensing systems, destroyers like the *Curtis Wilbur*, **which performed in the North Arabian Sea during Operation Enduring Freedom (above), can double as the communications hub for the fleet.**

ogy to fire artillery shells up to 63 miles inland.

Like the other branches of the military, the Navy will increase its use of unmanned aircraft and surface vessels in the 21st century. Employing this remote-controlled technology for surveillance and reconnaissance purposes at first, the Navy will eventually expand its role to include guard and combat duties. It's a brave new world indeed.

WORKHORSES [SHIPS]

FROM THE IRONCLAD TO THE BATTLESHIP TO TODAY'S CARRIERS, THE NAVY HAS ALWAYS RELIED ON SINGLE, CENTRAL WORKHORSES, SUPPORTED AND AUGMENTED BY NUMEROUS OTHER STANDBYS.

THE MODERN U.S. NAVY was born off Norfolk, Virginia, on March 8, 1862, when the 10-gun Confederate ship CSS *Virginia* attacked the 50-gun Union frigate USS *Cumberland*—the most powerful ship in the Union fleet. The *Cumberland* scrambled to reply, firing volleys of cannonballs back at the *Virginia*, but they all simply bounced off the sides of the Confederate ship—because the *Virginia* was one of the first ships built entirely of iron. Sailing right through the artillery fire, the *Virginia* rammed and sank the wooden *Cumberland*, then set the USS *Congress* afire, and drove aground the USS *Minnesota*.

The following day, the Union's first ironclad, the USS *Monitor*,

SSN-705/ SSBN

The U.S. Navy deploys two types of submarines, fast-moving attack-class vessels, such as the USS *City of Corpus Christi* SSN-705 (left), and ballistic missile subs, such as the SSBN (above).

Spotlight   USS JOHN C. STENNIS

One of the U.S. Navy's latest and greatest workhorses is the USS *John C. Stennis* CVN-74, an aircraft carrier built in the 1990s. The *Stennis* (above) weighs 97,000 tons and carries two nuclear reactors that give her a striking power limited only by the weapon stores she has on board or can procure from other sources. The centerpiece of a Navy battle group, the *Stennis* holds 3 million gallons of fuel for her aircraft and her healthy contingent of escort ships.

Her flight deck measures 1,092 feet long and carries 80 of the deadliest aircraft known to mankind (including F-18 and F-14 fighter jets, some of which are transported in the ship's interior). From the deck of the massive carrier, steam catapults launch the jets, which are trapped when they land by four sets of arresting gear.

The *Stennis*, which has been called a floating city, has 18 decks rising 24 stories into the air. The truth is, she's actually more of a small town, and one with few windows: The vessel carries a contingent of 5,000 service personnel, all of whom live belowdecks. There's a library onboard, as well as a gym, a few restaurants, a store, a post office, and even a jail.

Built to last 50 years into the 21st century, the USS *John C. Stennis* is 4.5 acres of American soil that can cruise at top speed to any location in the world (the carrier's maximum speed is classified, but it can travel in excess of 30 knots). And when a nation sees a modern U.S. aircraft carrier beelining for its shores, it pays attention.

CV-60

Among the aircraft carrier's many duties as the U.S. Navy's pivotal workhorse is to make a purposeful show of force, as the USS *Saratoga* (CV-60) demonstrates off the coast of Libya.

steamed to Norfolk and attacked the fixed-gun *Virginia*. Maneuvering low in the water, with the only two guns it owned swiveling on a movable turret, the *Monitor* pounded away at the *Virginia*. And the *Virginia* pounded back. The battle raged for four and a half hours. Finally, battered and beaten, the *Virginia* withdrew. But with that classic naval battle, a new era dawned. Every wooden ship was thereafter obsolete, and the age of the steel ship loomed near.

In most of the world's navies, the ironclad grew into the battleship, and the battleship reigned supreme as the workhorse of the navy, which is why the Japanese struck Pearl Harbor

with such force and determination. By robbing the U.S. of her battleships, Japan thought, America would be in no shape to fight an ocean war. But during that day of infamy, when the Japanese crippled most of the U.S. battleship fleet, the carriers *Saratoga*, *Lexington*, and *Enterprise* were out to sea. They would prove to be vital components of the modern U.S. Navy, and their survival ensured that America, whose ire had been fully inflamed by the attack, was still very much capable of waging war.

Admirals who had once sworn by the battleship now had to learn to use aircraft carriers. Their mixed squadrons of fighters and bombers enabled naval commmanders to reach from a great distance to destroy an enemy's ships. Carriers grew in importance while the battleship receded into the background.

After the Second World War, the British

DD-990

The USS *Ingersoll* (DD-990), a *Spruance*-class destroyer, cruises off the coast of Southern California. Powered by gas turbine engines, *Spruance*-class destroyers will be in service well into the 21st century.

began building their carriers with two airstrips at slight angles to each other atop the deck, a feature the Americans quickly adopted. The old-fashioned straight deck allowed only one operation at a time: takeoff or landing. The new deck permitted aircraft to take off from the bow while other planes landed on the stern. During the 1960s, carriers were fitted with nuclear reactors to extend their range infinitely. Today, a carrier forms the center of a naval task force; it is concentrically ringed by nearly every type of ship in the fleet except ballistic missile submarines (so far as we civilians know). Given their size, expense, and significant radar signature, modern carriers make a massive target. Their defense must be a priority.

To that end, the task force includes destroyers. Today's destroyers are small and fast (in excess of 30 knots), and many carry guided missiles. They mainly attack enemy submarines stalking carriers, but they have other roles as well. They can participate in surface action, resupply, and amphibious assaults, acting as protector and escort to the other ships involved in those missions. The guided-missile destroyers can also take on enemy aircraft and surface forces.

Many of the U.S. Navy's current destroyers are *Spruance*-class destroyers, which are driven by gas turbine engines—the first large U.S. warships so propelled. In 2002, 24 ships in the class were being upgraded with vertical launchers and new helicopter capabilities, among other improvements. The Navy expects *Spruance*-class destroyers to remain active well into the 21st century.

Also essential to the defense of carriers are the cruisers, most of which are named after famous U.S. battles. Today's $1-billion cruiser comes equipped with a host of weapons, including Tomahawks and Aegis-guided missiles. Aegis is a computer-controlled radar system perfectly suited to such multi-mission roles as anti-air, anti-surface, and anti-submarine warfare. And that makes the cruiser not only useful for escorting carriers, but also for taking care of amphibious forces, for operating independently, or as a flagship of surface-action groups.

Beneath the surface, of course, the Navy's workhorse is the submarine, which has been a

part of the inventory for more than 100 years. Most of the 20th century's subs were diesel- and battery-powered, and they proved deadly to just about any enemy warship that got in their way. Today, they are nuclear-powered, and their role is to encircle the carrier battle group at a great distance to provide early detection against any threats.

Beyond that role, the American strategy for submarines in the next century is to maintain technical superiority over numerical superiority.

The way the U.S. Navy hopes to do that is by developing ever more silent nuclear submarines that rarely have to surface. Currently, there are two types of submarines: attack submarines and ballistic-missile submarines. The former includes the *Seawolf* class and the *Virginia* class. Attack subs are meant to seek and destroy enemy ships and submarines, collect intelligence, and deliver special forces troops such as SEALs to strike zones. They are equipped with eight MK-48 torpedoes, and the *Seawolf* class can also fire Tom-

LCAC

Displaying its considerable freight capacity and impressive speed, one of the Marines' Landing Craft Air Cushions (above) flies toward the beach at Litohoro, Greece, during NATO's intervention in Kosovo. After landing in the early morning hours of June 10, 1999, members of the 26th Marine Expeditionary Unit (opposite) unload the gear for their mission.

ahawk cruise missiles at enemy troops and equipment on land.

Ballistic-missile submarines, which are named for U.S. states, are designed to be the third prong of the nuclear trident, with intercontinental ballistic missiles and nuclear bombers. *Ohio*-class ballistic missile subs can hold up to 24 Trident II D-5 missiles, and the older models are being retrofitted for the same purpose. These submarines silently and secretly cruise long distances under the sea and all around the world,

capable of firing their missiles on enemy targets at a moment's notice.

Aside from sending out aircraft carriers to provide a powerful base of operations off the coast of any nation, the Navy is also responsible for delivering assault forces into combat zones. For this task, it has the world's largest fleet of primary landing ships, which resemble small, boxy aircraft carriers. Anchoring just off the enemy shores, the primary landing ship delivers the essential tools of assault: airplanes that take-off and land vertically, attack helicopters, and heavily armed U.S. Marines. To make their landing, the Marines ride in vessels dubbed Landing Craft Air Cushions (LCACs). Essentially huge hovercraft propelled by twin fans mounted on the rear, these modern assault ships replaced the old-fashioned Higgins Boat that thousands of soldiers rode ashore on D-Day.

Needless to say, these state-of-the-art landing craft are designed to be safer than the old Higgins Boat. Fully amphibious, the LCAC can travel at high speed over the water, which helps to retain the element of surprise in any assault and shortens the interval between trips from the beach back to the landing ships for more troops. LCACs can also land on almost any shore—at least 70 percent of the world's coastline. The Higgins Boat, by contrast, could land on only 20 percent of global coastlines. Even though it is a hovercraft, the LCAC can carry an impressive 60 to 75 tons. This means that in addition to troops, LCACs can deliver M-1 tanks and other heavy weapons systems, equipment, and cargo—just about everything the Marines need to gain a foothold on enemy ground. A true workhorse, the LCAC is to the Higgins Boat what the ironclad was to the wooden warship: a great leap forward

In Action

LCACs

Added to the U.S. Navy fleet in 1986, Landing Craft Air Cushions (LCACs) allow the U.S. military wide latitude in its approach to planning, organizing, and conducting missions. The LCAC, which rides a cushion of air 4 feet above the surface of the water, can attain speeds in excess of 40 knots and has a range of close to 300 nautical miles.

The craft has proved its considerable worth in combat and non-combat situations alike. During one 24-hour stretch of Operation Desert Storm in 1991, LCACs made 55 runs in high seas and winds to deliver critical equipment in support of 20,000 U.S. Marines. The boats also launched U.S. personnel and heavy equipment during NATO's Peacekeeping Mission in Kosovo in 1999. But the LCACs' greatest moment to date may have come in Operation Sea Angel, a humanitarian mission off the coast of Bangladesh in 1991. In the wake of Typhoon Marian, which generated 140-mph winds and a 20-foot tidal surge, the LCAC was the only vessel capable of delivering crucial aid to isolated Bangladeshi islands.

READY FOR DUTY

SWIFT, VERSATILE, AND EQUIPPED WITH THE VERY LATEST TECHNOLOGY, THE U.S. NAVY'S READY-FOR-DUTY VESSELS REFLECT A SHIFT IN FOCUS FROM BLUE WATER OPERATIONS TO COASTAL, BROWN WATER MISSIONS.

USS *OHIO/* TRIDENT

The USS *Ohio*, part of a class of subs whose payloads will be converted from Trident nuclear missiles (opposite) to conventional ones, surfaces in Alaskan waters.

NO MANEUVER BETTER ILLUSTRATES the Navy's new emphasis on coastal operations than the conversion of four Trident or *Ohio*-class nuclear submarines from vessels loaded with nuclear missiles to ships carrying conventional guided missiles.

During the Cold War, Trident submarines roamed the world's oceans, deep beneath the waves, and could destroy a Soviet city at the touch of a button. The 21st century mission for these missile boats will be to bring massive firepower to bear quickly, while operating in shallower waters

AAAV

Half speedboat, half tank, the Advanced Amphibious Assault Vehicle (AAAV) can transport as many as 18 Marines and can travel 29 mph on water and 45 mph on land, where it can deploy its 30-millimeter cannon.

near an adversary's coast. The stealthy nature of the submarine means an enemy won't know the vessel is there until it's too late to quell the threat.

The conversion program is ingenious in many respects. Beginning in 2004, the Navy will remove the 24 nuclear missiles from these subs and use 22 of the tubes to carry cruise missiles, loading seven missiles into each tube for a total of 154 per sub. That means that each of the converted 560-foot boomers will have more cruise missiles at its disposal than an entire carrier battle group. But unlike a fleet of surface ships, the new guided-missile submarines will be able to operate independently, slipping unseen into enemy waters at any time.

The remaining two tubes on these converted subs will be used as exit points for SEAL com-

mandos operating as frogmen or boarding a new mini-underwater vessel attached to the submarine, which would ferry them closer to shore.

With four subs slated for conversion, some other tubes might find specialized uses. Two of the four subs will probably use two tubes for special-ops troops. Some may use one tube for a missile-shaped unmanned underwater vehicle called Manta 2, which is now being tested. Manta 2 might be used for mine detection, for surveillance, or even as a lure to provoke a response from enemy diesel submarines. With this mix of missiles, troops, and specialized vehicles, each guided-missile submarine will be able to conduct an array of military operations independently.

The Navy's newest *Virginia*-class submarines will also operate in coastal waters. Described as a shadow in shallow water, the first of these new boats, the USS *Virginia*, will be commissioned in 2004. At 377 feet in length, the *Virginia* can be classified as a fast-attack boat, but it is a radical departure from its immediate predecessor, the *Seawolf* (a member of the *Seawolf-*

class of subs), which was designed for deep-water operations. The *Virgina* is only slightly longer than the *Seawolf* but its diameter (34 feet) is considerably smaller, which means it carries fewer torpedoes, four to the *Seawolf*'s eight. But an arsenal of 12 vertical-launching cruise-missile tubes helps compensate for the firepower disparity and, more to the point, provides a land-attack capability. The *Virginia* also comes with a novel cone wrapped around the screw propeller, providing the sub with a muffler. While very quiet, the *Virginia* is slightly slower than the *Seawolf* and cannot dive as deep. The *Virginia* will also be able to carry, piggyback-style, a 55-ton mini-sub that will be used by SEAL commandos.

The *Virginia* features several innovations inside the hull as well. The most noticeable of these is that the traditional periscope has been scrapped in favor of a digital video camera that will have better resolution than the human eye.

The *Virginia* has more computer power onboard than the *Seawolf* and *its* predecessor, a *Los Angeles*-class sub, combined. The additional computing power will be used to process data quickly from new sensors mounted on the sail and under the chin. These sensors are designed to find enemy ships and subs in shallow waters, where sonar reflections from the ocean floor, and the background noise of noncombatant surface ships pose significant problems for detection. That's not to say the *Seawolf*-class of subs is obsolete or even inflexible. The third and last (that is, most modern) *Seawolf* boat, the USS *Jimmy Carter*, has a new hull section that includes a docking bay for remotely operated vehicles (ROVs), which couldn't fit in the 21-inch torpedo tubes of previous *Seawolfs*. This addition gives the *Jimmy Carter* the ability to remotely reconnoiter coastal areas.

Skimming the water's surface in coastal areas, charged with the task of putting U.S. troops ashore, is a new class of ships called LPD-17. The USS *San Antonio*, the first of a dozen LPD-17 ships, will hit the water in 2003. The ships measure 684 feet in length and carry all of the gear Marines require to launch amphibious operations capable of impacting an enemy up to 200

THE CHINESE NAVY

Though the United States and China maintain relatively cordial diplomatic relations, any increase in tension between the two nations would have to be regarded very seriously. With more than 1 billion citizens and a political philosophy starkly opposed to that of America, China is a significant potential U.S. adversary.

Dubbed the People's Liberation Army (PLA), the Chinese military is geared toward land-based conflict but does not neglect its navy, which is the only one in the world that rivals the U.S.'s seagoing force—and is currently undergoing notable improvements. The PLA navy recently purchased two Russian-made Soveremenny destroyers equipped with nuclear-tipped cruise missiles, and it produced four new Luhu and Luhai destroyers of its own, both of which are capable of firing cruise missiles.

Yet the greatest potential threat to the United States from China's navy will most likely come from its submarine divisions. In the spring of 2001, a PLA navy *Ming*-class sub conducted underwater operations for more than a month before being detected by U.S. sensors. And perhaps even more unsettling to U.S. interests, the PLA navy is building new classes of attack subs (Type 093) and ballistic-missile subs (Type 094) that will be, in the words of a Pentagon official, "potent platforms." The Type 094 subs will be equipped with 16 long-range nuclear missiles.

miles inland. The LPD-17 ships are designed to operate singly or in clusters, with a top speed of 22 knots. Assault and supply craft carried onboard include Landing Craft Air Cushions (LCACs) capable of transporting 70 tons, a pair of V-22 Osprey vertical-liftoff aircraft or four CH-46 helicopters, and a new Advanced Amphibious Assault Vehicle (AAAV) that transports as many as 18 Marines.

Part speedboat and part tank, the AAAV is equipped with wheels and tracks that tuck inside its aluminum hull for water travel. This bit of streamlining combines with engines that deliver 2,700 horsepower to give the AAAV a top speed of 29 mph over water, a vast improvement over the 6 to 8 mph of previous landing craft. Once on land, the AAAV revs up to speeds of 45 mph, bringing a 30-mm cannon to bear on targets. A built-in ventilation system allows the AAAV to travel through poison gas or similar hazards without endangering the troops inside or, as the case may be, belowdecks.

Other notable features of the *San Antonio* include the first fiber-optic network aboard a ship, which, in addition to providing the structure for other systems, sends commands to an automated 30-mm gun that can hit small, high-speed targets at long range. The LPD-17's armaments also include missile launchers. The *San Antonio* also has a 24-person hospital ward with two operating rooms. And a final notable element of the LPD-17 class is a creature comfort for its crews: a computer-equipped, redesigned berth that allows the sailor to sit upright and send e-mails to family and friends.

As the Navy continues to shift to brown water operations, it's always on the lookout for effective technology and vessels. During the crisis in East Timor in 1999, a wave-piercing catamaran called the *Jervis Bay* caught the eye of the U.S. brass. Deployed by Australia, the *Jervis Bay* ferried 20,000 troops, 430 vehicles, and 5,600 tons of cargo during 107 problem-free trips between Dili

and Darwin. The catamaran has a range of 1,100 nautical miles and a top speed of 43 knots, and it can be configured for helicopter landings.

The Navy is experimenting with other high-speed catamarans as well, including the helicopter-capable HSV-X1, which can carry as many as 5,000 Marines, and the Australian-designed WestPac Express. Both will probably function as support craft.

In addition to augmenting its inventory of ready-for-duty vessels, the Navy is adding new capabilities to existing ships to upgrade their efficiency and lethality. Leading the way are the innovations set for Aegis destroyers. These warships are being outfitted with a new, more sensitive radar system as well as a new 5-inch gun that will expand their firepower inland (see Spotlight). Destroyers may also get some added firepower for dealing with close-range attacks. Possible options include the Millennium Gun, developed by Lockheed Martin and the Swiss firm Oerlikon Contraves. The Millennium Gun creates a wall of steel in a rapid multipart process. First, it fires a special 35-mm round. This round then instantly dispenses 152 subprojectiles, which form an expanding, cone-shaped phalanx that shreds its target. Capable of firing 1,000 rounds per minute, the Millennium can destroy small surface craft and even sea-skimming cruise missiles.

The Navy's newest *Nimitz*-class aircraft carriers, the *Ronald Reagan* and CVN-77, represent a modest upgrade to the line. The ninth and tenth carriers in the *Nimitz* class, they will be deployed in 2003 and 2008, respectively, and should operate to mid-century. The most noticeable difference in the new carriers is a bulbous bow that replaces the V-shaped bow of their predecessors. The new bow provides more buoyancy to the forward end of the ship and gives the flight deck extra lift. It's a small change, but considering the Navy's shift in focus to littoral operations, blue-water carriers shouldn't be expected to change much.

Spotlight — MK34 SUPER GUN

While the USS *Winston Churchill* (DDG 81) may seem to be merely the latest in the U.S. Navy's long line of *Arleigh Burke*–class destroyers, the ship is equipped with one significant innovation that separates it from its predecessors, whose line began in 1991. The *Winston Churchill* sports a new 5-inch, 62-caliber "super gun" (above, firing) that marks the beginning of a long-range capability not seen in naval guns since the days when battleships pounded the shore and each other with 16-inch guns.

The MK34 Mod 1 Gun Weapon System, as the *Churchill*'s new weapon is formally called, is a computerized cannon featuring touchscreen fire control that, among other impressive capabilities, can automatically recognize and select between antipersonnel and armor-piercing rounds.

That feature will provide the MK34 with substantial and varied firepower, but what will dramatically increase the gun's effectiveness is the arrival in 2005 of an extended-range guided missile (ERGM). Using a guidance system based on Global Positioning System (GPS) technology, the ERGM will be able to lock onto military targets as far as 63 miles inland. The current range for standard shells is about 13 miles.

The MK34's unprecedented accuracy and firepower will be achieved at great cost-effectiveness. If all goes according to plan, the MK34 will be able to precisely target armored vehicles and troops inland, thereby taking the place of million-dollar Tomahawk missiles. A 5-foot ERGM shell will cost about $60,000.

To cut costs even further without sacrificing much range, accuracy, or potency, the Navy is considering a "dumber" version of the ERGM. This less carefully guided missile would have a range of 21 miles but cost even less than the MK34's current shells.

CUTTING EDGE

WHILE THE NAVY OF THE FUTURE WILL CONTINUE TO RELY ON THE AIRCRAFT CARRIER, IT WILL COMPLEMENT THAT CENTERPIECE WITH AN ARRAY OF NEW AUXILIARY VESSELS GREAT AND SMALL, MANNED AND UNMANNED.

W HENEVER A CRISIS EMERGES anywhere in the world, the first question politicians ask is, Where's the nearest aircraft carrier? Nothing gets the attention of a potential adversary like an aircraft carrier pulling into his waters. The carrier, then, has a kind of hardball-diplomacy role to go along with its military function. That isn't going to change anytime soon. The question is whether or not the carrier itself will change dramatically.

The short-term answer is no. After a detailed analysis, Navy planners have concluded that a redesign of the carrier would be just too costly. So when the Navy's new CVNX carrier is finished in 2013, it won't look dramatically different from its predecessors. But there will be some improved

RV TRITON/ MOB

The British-made *RV Triton* (opposite) is the world's largest trimaran and a model for similar future U.S. craft; still in the conceptual phase, the Mobile Offshore Base, or MOB (above), would be a vessel of unprecedented scale, with an airstrip 2 kilometers long.

LEVIATHAN

Like its namesake, the *Leviathan* would be a giant of the sea, yet possess astonishing agility; the heavily armed battleship would also come equipped with squadrons of unmanned underwater and aerial vehicles.

be some improved details. One will be a newly designed nuclear power plant that draws on space-saving lessons learned by submariners. The new plant will significantly extend the carrier's ability to operate without worrying about re-supply ships. The other innovation will be a new electromagnetic aircraft launch-and-recovery system that works much like the mechanism that propels Japanese "bullet" trains. This system replaces the old steam catapult, which is not only heavier and bulkier but also contributes to wear and tear on the planes them-

selves. The new system will help keep more planes available for flying missions.

While U.S. carriers won't change significantly, other types of ships may be radically revamped in response to a new emphasis on brown-water operations in coastal regions. And at least one entirely new feature is under consideration for 21st century naval warfare. Anticipating a lack of cooperation from foreign countries for forward military bases, the U.S. Navy is considering the development of a mobile offshore base (MOB) that would dwarf carriers in size. The MOB would be comprised of semisubmersible, interlocking modules linked to form a flight deck 2 kilometers long. In addition to aircraft, the MOB would house an Army brigade of 3,000 troops along with the landing craft to send them ashore. The MOB would have 3 million square feet available for equipment storage and maintenance facilities and would store 10 million gallons of fuel. While many engineering issues need to be resolved, the MOB would be a vessel of unprecedented scale.

Another revolutionary element under consideration is a fleet of warships based on a triple hull, or trimaran, design. This type of design is attractive for a variety of reasons. Trimarans could operate in rough seas that would send most ships scurrying for the nearest port. They are also faster than conventional ships, use less fuel, and require smaller crews. And the extra hulls afford the critical center hull some protection against torpedoes.

Both the U.S. and British navies are already experimenting with what is currently the world's largest trimaran, the *RV Triton*. Built by Britain's Defense Evaluation and Research Agency, the *Triton* is 100 meters long, displaces 1,100 tons, and can attain a speed of 20 knots. It has already made a transatlantic voyage.

In addition to the *Triton*, the U.S. Navy has four trimarans on the drawing board: a patrol boat, a frigate, a corvette, and a 750-foot battleship called the *Leviathan*, which would dwarf the *Triton* and possibly outperform it as well.

Despite its size, the *Leviathan* would be able to turn on a dime, thanks to side-mounted thrusters called azipods, which are also useful for docking. Firepower for the *Leviathan* would include two electromagnetic rail guns, powered

Spotlight — SUPERCAVITATING TORPEDO

Submarines generally attempt to get close enough to a target to strike it, but not so close that the enemy becomes aware of their presence. An approach currently in development would eliminate the need to balance these two factors. Deploying a supercavitating torpedo (right), which can travel 15 kilometers in 10 seconds, would enable the U.S. Navy to strike the enemy before he knows what hit him. Current torpedoes have a range of a few thousand feet. Their progress is slowed by the very water they travel through, which can cause them to stop and sink before hitting a target.

A supercavitating torpedo gets its initial thrust from the sub's onboard rocket engine, then maintains its high speed by emitting a gas through nozzles in its nose. The gas envelops the projectile, encasing it inside a bubble of water vapor. Ocean water flows around the bubble, exerting almost no drag on the torpedo, which slams into its target at or near the speed of sound.

Directional control of the torpedo could be accomplished with the same type of thrust vectoring used on some jet fighters, but altering the missile's course without destroying its speed-preserving bubble remains a technical hurdle.

Researchers at the U.S. Naval Undersea Warfare Center have already launched a supercavitating torpedo that broke the sound barrier. And the Russian navy is said to have developed its own 200-mph version called Shkval, which is rumored to have been aboard the Kursk Oscar II-class submarine when it sank in the Barents Sea on August 12, 2000.

DD-21/ DD-X PROTOTYPES

The DD-21 stealth destroyer concept (left) was a precursor to the DD-X warship (above), which is scheduled to appear in 2011. Part of the Navy's Future Surface Combatant Program, the DD-X will be equipped with a gun capable of firing GPS-guided shells 63 miles inland as well as an electric-drive propulsion system to power onboard laser and microwave weapons. The destroyer will also possess the networking capability to coordinate artillery fire with other ships in the fleet.

by the ship's turbine engines. Each rail gun could fire an artillery shell 500 miles at speeds up to Mach 10, allowing it to quickly hit inland targets while the ship remains in international waters. Also onboard the mighty *Leviathan* would be an array of 80 unmanned underwater and aerial vehicles.

While the trimarans remain in the experi-

mental stage, a new line of destroyers, the DD-X-class, is on its way to production, spearheaded by Northrop Grumman. These new stealthy ships may vaguely resemble Civil War ironclads, but they include some decidedly 21st century technologies. Chief among these is an electric-drive propulsion system that also would be used as the power source for onboard laser and microwave weapons. The DD-X-class ships will also come equipped with an array of missiles and a 5-inch gun like the ones currently being deployed on new *Arleigh Burke*-class destroyers. These guns can fire GPS-guided shells 63 miles inland. Other goals for the DD-X program include a small crew size of about 100 sailors and a networking capability that integrates radar and coordinates artillery fire with other ships in the fleet. The DD-X-class is scheduled to debut in 2011, and the concept will be extended to develop a cruiser, the CG-X, for deployment in 2018.

Another harbinger of possible ships to come is the experimental littoral surface craft being built by the Office of Naval Research for a 2004 launch. The corvette-sized LSC-X is a high-speed (50 knots), shallow-draft (3 meters) craft designed for scooting around coastal waters. Initially, the hull will be of a simple catamaran design, but the Navy plans to add "lifting bodies" fore and aft that would partially elevate the hull out of the water. The lifting bodies, which could also carry fuel, would be coated with special polymers that reduce drag. Micro-bubbles would be injected into the water ahead of them to reduce drag even further. The LSC-X's missions would include anti-submarine warfare against diesel-powered vessels, and the insertion and extraction of special-operations troops. For this last function, the LSC-X would come equipped with a ramp at its stern that would allow rubber rafts to drive up onto the deck.

The LSC-X would also be the host ship for unmanned aerial vehicles and for the Spartan, an unmanned surface vessel (USV) the Navy is developing for reconnaissance, surveillance, and patrol duty. The Spartan will look like a powerboat with a winter cover thrown over the seats. A more advanced design calls for the construction of a USV that would look at home in a science-fiction movie. Called Phast, this U-shaped,

The Other Side

NAVAL TERRORISTS

Perhaps the gravest current threat to the global American naval presence is the so-called asymmetrical warfare being waged by international terrorists, most notably Al Qaeda. This point was driven home in awful fashion with the Al Qaeda-sponsored attack on the USS *Cole* destroyer as it refueled in a port in Yemen on October 12, 2000. Terrorists detonated explosives on a small boat next to the *Cole*, killing 17 U.S. sailors and injuring 39 while blowing a massive hole in the ship's side.

The technology used in that attack was far from cutting edge, but the tactics and techniques were diabolically so. The enemy analyzed the U.S. deployment, found its weakness, and attacked accordingly. Of course, the U.S. Navy took immediate and numerous steps to prevent such assaults in the future, including instituting proactive antiterrorist and force-protection measures, altering training, and reorganizing the way offices and agencies within the Department of Defense share intelligence. And intelligence is the most powerful weapon for fighting this sinister adversary, which the Department of Defense characterizes as "adaptive, persistent, patient, and tenacious."

CVNX

Set to appear in 2013, the CVNX carrier will not be a radical departure from its predecessors, though it will have a new, sleeker nuclear power plant, and an electromagnetic launch-and-recovery system for aircraft.

14.5-meter pod would lurk low in the water before elevating to attain speeds of up to 32 knots using its thruster pods.

The LSC-X fits into the "Streetfighter" concept of vessels advocated by Vice Admiral Arthur K. Cebrowski, the head of the Naval War College. Manned by a crew of only 13, Streetfighters would be a class of inexpensive, fast, heavily-armed catamarans that would probe enemy waters for submarines and other vessels. They would be networked together and, like the LSC-X, would rely on UAVs and USVs for reconnaissance. If one Streetfighter were attacked, the others would swarm on the attacker from all directions, relying on speed to fire their weapons and retreat before the enemy had a chance to return fire.

Unfortunately, in war games, simulated Streetfighters, which sound much like World War II PT boats, have proved easy to hit, and their crews faced almost certain death. But the Streetfighter idea continues to evolve. The Sea

Archer is a Streetfighter concept for a small, 600-foot catamaran-hulled carrier built exclusively for Unmanned Combat Aerial Vehicles (UCAVs). Dubbed Sea Arrows, these UCAVs could use the Streetfighter swarming tactics to attack an enemy vessel without running the risk of casualties. The Sea Arrows would weigh about 15,000 pounds each and be able to stay in the air for 8 hours. The Sea Archer carriers would be supported by another catamaran, the Sea Lance, which would have the same 45-knot speed as the Sea Archer and carry 51 "cells" for an array of short- and long-range missiles. The final element of the concept is Sea Quiver, a resupply ship.

Just as unmanned combat planes might dominate ocean airspace in the coming decades, armed, unmanned submarines may rule underwater. Manta is a concept for a 50-ton unmanned sub that would launch from a manned submarine and be able to operate autonomously if required. Four Mantas, in

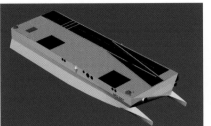

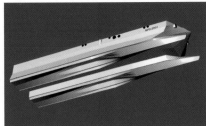

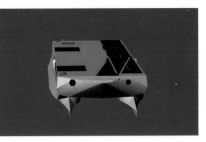

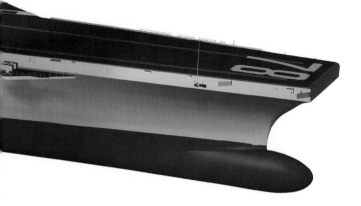

SEA ARCHER

Part of a conceptual group of unmanned naval combat technologies, the Sea Archer (above, from three angles) would be a 600-foot catamaran-hulled carrier for unmanned combat aerial vehicles dubbed Sea Arrows.

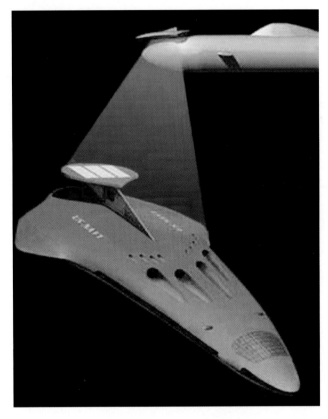

MANTA

The potential future of submarine warfare, the Manta (right) is a prototype for a 50-ton unmanned underwater vessel that, once launched from a mother sub, could operate autonomously and fire as many as eight torpedoes.

fact, could be fitted around the hull of a sub, forward of the sail. With a prototype already undergoing sea trials, the oval, plate-shaped Manta would house four full-size torpedoes or eight half-size torpedoes. These could be supercavitating missiles, which means they'd be faster than the speed of sound (see Spotlight), and they could also target enemy aircraft. Manta may also come equipped with a supercavitating gun that would shoot bullets at underwater mines or other targets. Super-cavitating bullets are already being used by helicopter crews for mine-clearing. The Navy envisions putting similar weapons below the waterline on ships for mine-clearing and as a defense against torpedo attacks.

Other unmanned underwater reconnaissance vehicles may not even appear to be vessels. In a development seemingly drawn from the latest James Bond thriller, Draper Laboratory in Cambridge, Massachusetts, has built an 8-foot, 300-pound robotic tuna that mimics the action of the fish. Equipped with sensors, or weapons, Draper's agile "tuna" could become the ultimate underwater covert operator—and yet another ingenious example of cutting-edge naval technology.

WEAPONRY

B Y THE END OF WORLD WAR I, the U.S. military's weaponry had come a long way from the flintlocks of the Revolution and the muzzle-loaded muskets and cannons of the Civil War.

With the machine gun waiting in the wings—indeed, that weapon was ready for duty well before it was officially adopted—the military's workhorse weapon was the M-1 Garand, named after its inventor, John Garand of the Springfield Armory in Massachusetts. The gas-operated Garand weighed 9.5 pounds and held a clip of eight .30-06-caliber rounds. It fired twice as fast as the American 1917 Enfield, a British weapon modified to fire American ammunition. The wooden-stock, semiautomatic Garand was rugged, easy to assemble, and highly accurate, and it could be loaded with the slap of a clip. The Garand did have two significant faults, though. The rifle kicked back brutally when fired, and the clip emitted a resonant *ping* when ejected, a telltale—and potentially fatal—signal to the enemy that the Garand's bearer was out of ammo and would need time to reload. Still, the M-1 saw action in every significant U.S. battle from the Kasserine Pass to the invasion of Okinawa, to Korea.

The first truly modern gun was not only a landmark advancement in armament technology, but also an American icon. Appearing in 1921, the Thompson Submachine Gun, or Tommy gun, quickly became a fixture in gangland and Hollywood alike, but not, curiously, in the military or law enforcement arsenals. Images of gangsters spraying Tommy gun rounds out the windows of speeding black sedans dominated both movie-theater screens and newspaper pages, but the U.S. military was reluctant to spend money on a newfangled weapon that had yet to be battle-tested.

The Tommy gun was simply ahead of its time. With a clip of 20, 30, or 50 rounds of

.45-caliber ammo, the 7-pound submachine gun could fire 50 shots per minute and was deadly at short range. The Marines used the Tommy for close-range combat in the jungles of Nicaragua in 1927 and, impressed with its performance, officially adopted the gun in 1930. The Army didn't make the Thompson a standard part of its arsenal until 1936, and by the time World War II started, the weapon had been surpassed by its German counterparts. Going back to the drawing board, the Thompson's manufacturers created the M-1 Carbine in 1942. The most ubiquitous U.S. weapon of World War II, the M-1 was extremely lightweight (5 pounds) and fired a clip of 15 rounds of .30-caliber ammo. The Carbine was accurate, with a light recoil, but it often required multiple hits to drop an enemy soldier.

Another workhorse weapon of World War II was the Browning .30-Caliber Air-Cooled Machine Gun. After undergoing a series of modifications, the Browning went on to serve in Korea and Vietnam as well. At 41 pounds, it was heavy, but it could fire as many as 550 rounds per minute. The Browning could be mounted on a vehicle or carried by a soldier; in the former capacity, the .30-cal. could attack a specific target or sustain suppressive fire. It became a very effective offensive weapon.

After the Korean conflict, the military sought to replace or improve most of the weapons in its inventory. The M-1 Carbine gave way to the M-16, a weapon still in use today. The M-16 is complex and composed of many parts, and soldiers in Vietnam were always cleaning it—as many as

SQUAD AUTOMATIC WEAPON

A Marine fires his Squad Automatic Weapon (SAW) during a practice session outside a U.S. Marine base in southern Afghanistan in December 2001. The SAW is one of the U.S. military's new workhorse weapons.

three times a day. Its firepower, however, is enormous: 700 to 950 rounds per minute. Three 20-round clips of its 5.56mm ammunition can carve a hole the size of a man in a cinderblock wall. And the M-16 packs its firepower in a light frame—it weighs a mere 7 pounds. The Navy SEALs, one of the military's elite units, still use the M-16, and when they attach the 44mm M-203 grenade launcher to it, the M-16 makes quite an impression on 21st century enemy forces.

WORKHORSES

FROM THE POWERFUL BUT TROUBLED M-16 TO THE STATE-OF-THE-ART M-249, WORKHORSE WEAPONS CAN BE THE DIFFERENCE BETWEEN LIFE AND DEATH FOR THE SOLDIER IN THE FIELD.

O F ALL THE GEAR A SOLDIER carries into battle, nothing is more important to his survival than his weaponry. Today, the U.S. infantry's standard-issue rifle remains the Colt M-16, a rapid-fire weapon that began service in 1963. First orders for the rifle that year were massive: 85,000 of them for the Army and 19,000 for the Air Force. By 1966, as the Vietnam War became an entrenched conflict, the Army had ordered another 200,000 units.

On paper, the M-16 seems to be the perfect weapon. It weighs slightly less than 7 pounds and can fire in either cyclical, automatic, or semi-

M-249/ M-16

The M-249 Squad Automatic Weapon (opposite) has none of the glitches of the M-16 (above), which, despite an array of problems, has been the military's workhorse rifle since the 1960s.

automatic modes. It holds 20- to 30-round magazines, pairs of which, during combat, soldiers tape end-to-end for quick reloading. The M-16's rounds are only .22-caliber, but since the gun can fire 700 to 950 rounds per minute (rpm) in cyclical mode, 150 to 200 rpm in automatic mode, and 45 to 65 rpm as a semiautomatic, its bursts tend to be fatal. The M-16 has a range of 400 meters, though at that distance accuracy suffers slightly. Soldiers find it most effective at a range of about 200 meters. Whatever the distance, though, the M-16, which incorporates "in-line" recoil to keep the barrel from wandering off target during firing, is among the most accurate in the world.

Despite these impressive features, and despite its long service, the M-16 has not been without its glitches, some of them significant. To keep the gun lightweight, its designers gave it a hammer that operates by gas pressure. Soldiers must keep the gun's gas tubes and chamber as clean as a dinner plate or the gun will not function properly. This proved to be an almost impossible task in the muck and dust of South Vietnam. Bullet manufacturers further complicated matters during the war when they issued a new type of gunpowder that left gobs of calcium carbonate in the gas tube. In response, the army issued rifle-cleaning kits, which included a barrel-cleaning rod. Still, soldiers' guns frequently jammed during intense firefights with the enemy. Eventually, the military adopted an M-16 with a chrome chamber, which didn't eliminate the problem but made the gun easier to clean.

The Vietnam-era M-16 also had a spring-loading mechanism that wasn't as strong as it needed to be and became another source of jamming. If you loaded it with a 30-round magazine, the gun would almost certainly seize up. Through trial and sometimes fatal error, the grunts learned to fill their magazines with 27 rounds, which greatly reduced jamming.

Finally, the M-16 lacks a shoulder strap. Some soldiers have modified their weapons with a sling, but to this day, the military has not seen fit to equip the M-16 with this most basic feature, leav-

M-4

Currently the weapon of choice for Special Forces teams throughout the world, the M-4 gets most of its parts from the M-16, but it is shorter, comes with a "red aiming reference," and is better suited to short-range combat.

ing troops to carry the gun by the crude handle on top of the weapon.

Even with all of its shortcomings, though, the M-16 can be a devastating weapon. Its immediate descendant, the M-4 carbine, gets more than 80 percent of its parts from the M-16. The M-4 is

currently the weapon of choice for Special Forces teams throughout the world. Shorter than an M-16 and with a forward handgrip, the M-4 is ideal for short-range combat. It has an M-68 sight, also known as a "red aiming reference" (read: small red dot), that shows exactly where the bullet will strike. Small wonder the Special Forces like it.

Though the M-4 comes with a bipod mount, the absence of a modern version of the Browning Automatic Rifle led military brass to commission the M-249 .22-caliber Squad Automatic Weapon (SAW). Adopted in 1982, the SAW tips the scales at a relatively lightweight 22 pounds fully loaded, and it fires 200-round belts at between 750 and 900 rounds per minute. A comforting fact for those depending on the weapon in battle is that the M-249 will accept disintegrating belts and can even fire the M-16's 30-round magazines if need be. According to soldiers who've used the weapon, the M-249 can fire roughly 10,000 rounds without being cleaned. Still, the typical Marine carries an extra chrome-lined barrel that he can attach in 3 seconds.

Mounted atop the old Browning Automatic

Rifle tripod, the M-249 can be fired from a prone position, but it also can be fired from the hip or from a kneeling position. Fired from the prone position, the SAW can mow down enemy troops with lethal force. And like your postman, the SAW will work in almost any conditions: The gun can fire in temperatures as high as 155° F and as low as minus 50° F; it can function after falling into water, and it can blaze away in the dust and heat of the desert, in the humidity of the jungle, and in the

M-249

A U.S. Special Forces soldier keeps his M-249 Squad Automatic Weapon at the ready during a military training exercise in Basilan province, the Philippines, in March 2002. The SAW can fire as many as 900 rounds per minute.

mud. Its rounds are only .22-caliber, but they can penetrate an old U.S. Army steel helmet at 470 meters.

After the rifle, the soldier's primary weapons are the family of hand grenades he carries into

Spotlight

AT-4 ANTITANK WEAPON

What do you do when a main battle tank or armored personnel carrier is plowing right toward your position? If you're a Marine, you reach for your AT-4 antitank weapon. Manufactured by FFV Ordnance, Sweden, and Alliant Techsystems, the AT-4 (below) represents a departure of sorts for the U.S. military. It's one of a handful of weapons in the modern American arsenal designed outside the U.S. (The others are the Hawker AV-8 Harrier aircraft and the Martin B-57, a tactical bomber first known as the British Electric Canberra.)

Forty inches long and weighing 14.75 pounds, the AT-4 is a thoroughly devastating weapon. It can penetrate 400 millimeters—15.75 inches—of rolled homogeneous armor. The AT-4 has a bore of 84 millimeters and fires a rocket with a shaped-charge warhead. While its maximum effective range is slightly less than 984 feet, the warhead travels that distance in less than 1 second. Picture that for a moment. Tests show that the AT-4 can operate in temperatures between 140° F and minus 104° F, which makes it serviceable for fighting on any continent.

What's more, unlike the two-man bazooka, the AT-4 antitank weapon can be fired off the shoulder of a single soldier. And its cost of $1,480 is a small price to pay for a weapon that can stop the largest tank in any enemy's arsenal.

combat. First of these is the M-67 fragmentation grenade, which weighs 14 ounces and carries 6.5 ounces of explosives. The average soldier can throw an M-67 about 40 meters. The grenade will kill anyone within roughly 5 meters of where it lands, injure people up to 15 meters away, and blast fragments to a distance of 250 meters.

To mark a position, soldiers use the M-18 colored smoke grenade. This device weighs 19 ounces and carries 11.5 ounces of colored smoke mixture, including violet, green, red, and yellow.

M14 TH3 Incendiary. This grenade has a light sheet-metal body filled with 26.5 ounces of thermate. A precursor of this substance, dubbed thermite, filled World War II-era grenades. The improved thermate burns at some 4,000° F, soldering together any metal parts with which it comes in contact. The grenade burns for 40 seconds and will produce a hole in a plate of half-inch steel. Since thermate produces its own oxygen, AN-M14 grenades will also burn under water. Ideally, a soldier could lay a thermate grenade on a cannon's breech or tumble one down a barrel, or place it on an aircraft or on almost any other item he seeks to render ineffective, but he could also sling the grenade up to 80 feet to good effect.

Whether they're slinging grenades or firing 750 rounds per minute, U.S. soldiers are there to do business, and their workhorse weaponry, warts and all, serves them well.

M-67/AN-M14 INCENDIARY
U.S. Sergeant Timothius Robinson (left) lobs an M-67 grenade during a training exercise in Queensland, Australia. American soldiers used thermate AN-M14 Incendiary grenades (below) to clear caves in Afghanistan.

The M-18's canister has five emission holes and produces smoke for up to 90 seconds. Troops can hurl it about 35 meters.

More potent than the M-67, and used to disable enemy heavy equipment, such as cannons, tanks, or armored personnel carriers, is the AN-

READY FOR DUTY

FASTER, LIGHTER, MORE POWERFUL, AND MORE ACCURATE THAN THEIR PREDECESSORS, THE MILITARY'S READY-FOR-DUTY WEAPONS REPRESENT THE BULWARK OF COMBAT TECHNOLOGY.

TRAP T-2/ XM-777

As part of the military's general shift toward unmanned technology, the Army is evaluating the Trap T-2 remote-controlled weapons platform (above). The new XM-777 Howitzer (opposite) is 6,500 pounds lighter than its famous predecessor but packs just as much power and range.

A BAND OF ENEMY SOLDIERS digs in behind a wall, like ticks on a deer, and lays a curtain of machine-gun fire down the street. Three hundred meters away, a squad of U.S. soldiers takes cover; if they were stick their heads out for a look, it would be tantamount to suicide. But such a move is not necessary. One of the Americans pokes his rifle around the corner of a building. The gunsight on his rifle is also a 6X night-vision-capable video camera that allows the soldier to zoom in on the enemy's position. The camera relays images to the soldier through a wire connected to the display mounted on his helmet visor.

He decides that the 30 rounds of 5.56mm ammunition in his magazine will have little effect on the well-entrenched enemy. His gun has two bar-

VIDEO-CAMERA GUNSIGHT
New U.S. rifles will come with night-vision-capable video-camera sights that will allow soldiers to observe adversaries without putting themselves in harm's way.

rels—a smaller one mounted underneath a larger one—but only one trigger. The soldier flicks a switch on his rifle. A laser rangefinder measures the distance to the target and communicates the data to a computer chip built into the fuse of a

20mm high-explosive (HE) shell loaded into the rifle's larger barrel. Using buttons placed around the trigger guard, the soldier can set the HE round to detonate in front of, above, or behind a target. He can also set the shell to explode on impact or after a short delay, if, for example, he wants the round to burst through a window before exploding on its target.

With his current enemy down the street and behind a wall, the soldier decides to detonate the

Inventor

O'DWYER VLE

The world's first entirely electronic handgun, the O'Dwyer VLE pistol is named for its inventor, Mike O'Dwyer, the president and chief executive officer of Australian ballistics technology company Metal Storm, which produced the VLE.

O'Dwyer assumed his post at Metal Storm in 1994, and he has been working on the company's electronic ballistics technology since the early 1980s. He continues to refine his invention for an increasingly wide array of applications and has introduced it to the defense departments of Australia, the United States, and the United Kingdom.

The VLE, which stands for Variable Lethality Law Enforcement, can fire a three-shot burst in 1/500th of a second, which works out to 60,000 rounds per minute. "The VLE prototype has no conventional magazine. The bullets are stacked in-line in the barrel, ready to fire, with the pistol grip containing three sets of electronics," Mr. O'Dwyer said. "One set controls the firing operation of the weapon, another provides audio and visual confirmation of weapons settings, and a third manages and limits access to the weapon."

With no moving parts, save bullets, the O'Dwyer is an example of science fiction transformed into science fact.

HE round above the target. He squeezes the trigger, feeling very little recoil despite the size of the shell. A veteran of several previous campaigns, the soldier knows that his chances of hitting the target are 40 percent better than with the grenade launcher he formerly used. Still, the soldier fires a second HE round for good measure. That one also detonates in the air above the wall, raining shrapnel down on its victims. The HE shrapnel can pierce light armor. All is quiet

from the enemy position down the street.

The soldier's versatile and potent weapon is called the Objective Individual Combat Weapon (OICW), a slightly ponderous name for a weapon designed to replace the M-16 and the M-4 as the military's workhorse rifle. The OICW, which is scheduled for deployment in 2009, is 33 inches long and weighs 12 pounds. Its HE rounds—which will replace the grenade launcher that currently attaches to M-16s—have

OICW/HE ROUNDS

The Objective Individual Combat Weapon (above), scheduled for deployment in 2009, fires 20mm high-explosive, or HE, rounds (left) that can be programmed to denotate in front of, above, or behind a target.

a range of 1,000 meters. The soldier can fire 10 HE rounds per minute. The 5.56mm portion of the gun has about the same range as an M-16 and fires at the same rate. Other features include an electronic compass, direct-view optics, an automatic target tracker, and a heat-seeking thermal capability.

In tandem with the OICW, the Pentagon is developing the Objective Crew Served Weapon (OCSW), a replacement for the venerable .50-caliber machine gun. The 37-pound OCSW, which requires a two-man crew, uses a laser rangefinder for precise targeting of two types of 25mm ammunition out to 2,000 meters.

One round is a high-explosive shell for use against ground troops. The other is an armor-piercing bullet for use against vehicles. The OCSW fires as many as 260 rounds per minute, with bullets reaching maximum range in slightly less than 9 seconds.

Another weapon that may soon be available is the Advanced Sniper Rifle. While details about the gun are scarce, DARPA worked with an Australian company called Metal Storm Limited to develop a new firing system. The Advanced Sniper Rifle would use a system that "pre-loads" the barrel as a means of reducing the number of mechanical steps required to load, fire, eject, and reload. Metal Storm's special bullets expand and lock into place within the barrel in response to high pressure immediately ahead of the bullet. This means that as one bullet fires, the next bullet in the stack stays put.

Another advantage of this technology is that the shooter can electronically control and vary the rate of fire. Metal Storm claims that its guns could fire at speeds of up to 1 million rounds per minute. The technology could be adapted for use in the OCSW and the OICW.

Metal Storm Limited is also shooting hand-gun technology into the computer age with its O'Dwyer VLE gun, the world's first electronic pistol. Reminiscent of the "Lawgivers" that the police in the sci-fi film *Judge Dredd* used, the seven-shot O'Dwyer can fire multiple rounds with a single pull of the trigger. The weapon also audibly and electronically confirms firing settings, and its owner wears a dress ring containing a security transponder that the gun will recognize to the exclusion of all others. The pistol can fire a three-round burst in 1/500th of a second, effectively turning the slowest cowpoke

Spotlight — THE HORNET

An enemy convoy of tanks and trucks makes its way down a dirt road, comfortable in the knowledge that U.S. forces have not been seen in the vicinity for weeks. Unbeknownst to them, though, American troops have left behind a new, remote-controlled munition called the Hornet. The enemy convoy is about to feel its sting.

Equipped with seismic and acoustic sensors that can detect both the vibrations and the sound of moving vehicles, the Hornet (right) calculates speed and direction and uses its onboard library to determine the types of vehicles passing by. Advanced electronics and GPS navigation receivers allow one Hornet to communicate this information to other Hornets in the field. When a declared target enters the Hornet's 100-meter range, the weapon rotates, tilts, and launches an explosive projectile above the enemy vehicle. An infrared sensor onboard the warhead homes in on the vehicle, aiming for the top of a tank, for example, where armor is usually the thinnest.

The Hornet is essentially a smart mine, and it can be turned off (again, by remote control) to allow the passage of friendly forces through the area, or at the cessation of hostilities. This last feature eliminates the threat of casualties among civilian noncombatants—the bane of war-torn areas throughout the world.

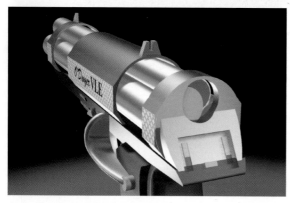

O'DWYER VLE

The world's first electronic pistol, the seven-shot O'Dwyer VLE (above, illustrated from three angles) can fire multiple rounds with a single pull of the trigger and has a built-in security system that prevents anyone but authorized operators from firing it.

in the corral into a Jesse James-style shooter. The company is also developing a compact, multiple-barrel, 24-shot weapon that will allow the shooter to switch between lethal and non-lethal ammo as needed.

Another Metal Storm project uses the same technology as a replacement for mines buried underground. Called the Area Denial Weapon System, it consists of multiple-barrel pods with a range of lethal and nonlethal ammo as well as various sensors and cameras. It can monitor a protection zone automatically or with a remote operator who can determine the level of response required. The system is portable and can be programmed to self-destruct so it won't be a danger to civilians when hostilities end.

A similarly compact and portable weapon is Spike, a small guided missile currently nearing deployment. The 4-pound missile and its 5-pound launcher can be carried in a backpack and would be used by Special Operations Forces and light infantry. Spike's gunner will use the weapon's electro-optical TV tracker to lock on to a target from as far as 2 miles away—well beyond the range of unguided weapons like the grenade launchers (150 yards) or .50-caliber machine guns (1,200 yards) an enemy might use in defense. The team of four Spike operators would carry a total of six missiles into battle. Each $4,000 Spike has enough punch to destroy a non-armored target, which, according to military estimates, includes 80 percent of the targets on a battlefield.

Spike may be available for use as soon as 2003 and would supplement larger, more expensive ready-for-duty weapons like the anti-tank Javelin and the anti-aircraft Stinger missiles, which are also portable. The military may also deploy Spike on ships and unmanned aerial drones.

As the military looks toward a future replete with unmanned aircraft, vessels, and ground vehicles, it is also investigating remotely operated weapons for perimeter defense or special operations. A good example of this technology is Tacti-

cal Telepresent Technologies' TRAP T-2 platform, which can be adapted for several types of rifles. The TRAP T-2 comes with a video-camera sight linked to computer targeting software that quickly calibrates range, wind, and target movement. Operating the TRAP T-2 with a joystick, soldiers will be able to fire and reacquire new targets in less than a second. Another appealing feature of remote-controlled weapons technology is that it can use a computer to link multiple guns together— and enable a single operator to fire them all.

Of all the ready-for-duty weapons, though, none is more eagerly anticipated than the XM-777 Howitzer, an extremely powerful automatic due in 2003. The gun can fire a .39-caliber round 18.9 miles, but even more appealing than that capability is the XM-777's relatively light weight. It checks in at 9,500 pounds, which might seem heavy to the casual observer but is considerably lighter than the 16,000-pound M-198 Howitzer the XM-777 replaces. British Aerospace built the new Howitzer with lightweight titanium, which

AREA DENIAL SYSTEM

Conceived as a replacement for subterranean mines, the Area Denial Weapon System is a portable, remote- or automatically-controlled machine that can fire lethal or nonlethal ammunition from its multiple-barrel pods.

dropped its weight and greatly increased its mobility. Soldiers will use the tow hook under the XM-777's muzzle to attach the gun to a 5-ton truck and make a swift advance or departure. Further, the CH-46 helicopter or the MV-22 tilt-rotor Osprey will be able to carry the newly lightweight Howitzer into battle, so a fast-moving infantry won't have to worry about leaving its artillery support behind. The new Howitzer also comes with an updated firing system that doubles the firing speed of the previous model from 4 to 8 rounds per minute, with a GPS receiver and a ballistics computer system to improve accuracy.

Like the rest of the ready-for-duty weaponry, the new Howitzer helps create a more effective and better-protected infantry.

CUTTING EDGE

THE MILITARY IS CURRENTLY RESEARCHING A VAST RANGE OF CUTTING-EDGE WEAPONRY, FROM HIGH-POTENCY FIREARMS TO MICROWAVE WEAPONS, TO NONLETHAL OPTIONS INVOLVING SOUND AND LIGHT.

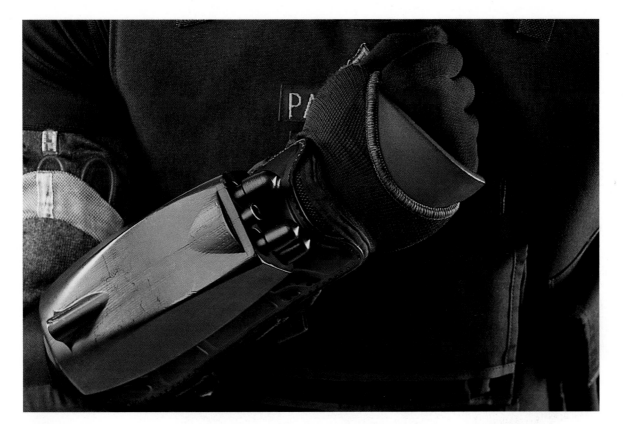

DRESSED IN A BLACK, form-fitting uniform and what looks like a matching motorcycle helmet, the U.S soldier of the year 2025 resembles a kind of high-tech ninja warrior. Or so thinks the urban guerrilla who glimpsed the American while hiding in the shadows atop a small building. It will be one of the guerrilla's last thoughts, for unknown to him, the U.S soldier he's seen is not alone. No, the American is the leader of a squad, and he has seized the high ground, a rooftop some 1,000 meters away. Thanks to a zoom camera mounted in his helmet and a wireless network link, he has spotted the guerrilla and relayed the image of the enemy not only to the visor displays of his squad members but also to U.S. military headquarters.

FUTURE WARRIOR/ WEAPONS POD

A soldier models the Future Warrior system (opposite), which featured a four-barreled weapons pod (above) in its original incarnation.

U.S. military brass confirms the identity of the guerrilla against a database of known suspects and grants the squad leader permission to fire. He has the most direct shot, but at this range, standard ammo would be ineffective. Undeterred, the squad leader extends his arm, angling his hand downward. Strapped to his forearm like a fearsome black hawk is a weapons pod. The squad leader watches his visor-mounted display as a bull's-eye appears superimposed on the enemy. He whispers, "Fire on target," and the voice-activated weapon launches one of its four 15-millimeter projectiles from his forearm with a small whoosh.

But the guerrilla's sixth sense somehow alerts him to the danger, and he takes off running, firing his automatic rifle wildly. No matter; the squad leader's projectile is equipped with tiny heat-seeking sensors, which have locked on to the target. The chase is a short one. Exploding like a hand grenade, the projectile sends shrapnel in every direction. Even a last-

FUTURE WARRIOR HELMET

The U.S. soldier of the future will wear a sleek, motorcycle-style helmet equipped with a zoom camera, a 360-degree microphone, and a visor display. The helmet will also be linked to a wireless network.

second dodge would have been useless for the guerrilla.

The team leader's weapons pod has lately been replaced by a four-barreled, handheld firearm with the same capabilities, but this vision of the future, which is already on the drawing board at the U.S. Army's Soldier Systems Center in Natick, Massachusetts, otherwise remains the same. In addition to its heat-seeking mini-rockets, the firearm would hold a clip of 4.6-mm bullets for close encounters of the deadliest kind. At the heart of the weapon is a group of microelectromechanical thrusters that launch the projectiles. The military envisions using this weapon mostly in urban combat—a likely location for future conflicts, given that cities are growing in population every year—but it would work effectively in jungle, desert, and rural environments as well.

Such a firearm would bring a lethal finality to the battlefield, but in the future, the emphasis may actually shift to nonlethal weapons

FOUR-BARRELED FIREARM

The Future Warrrior system's four-barreled firearm, which replaces the weapons pod of the earlier prototype, will be an extraordinarily lethal gun, capable of firing 15-millimeter heat-seeking mini-rockets, as well as 4.6-millimeter bullets for close-range combat.

that incapacitate rather than destroy an adversary. The nonlethal option could be an important tool that, among other uses, provides an opportunity to interrogate enemies associated with shadowy terrorist organizations. Nonlethal weapons may also be the only legitimate option in conducting future peacekeeping or humanitarian missions in which casualties are politically unacceptable. They would also reduce casualties among noncombatants who get caught in the crossfire of an urban firefight.

One nonlethal weapon could employ sound as an incapacitating force. Inaudible, low-frequency sound waves may be able to disrupt the body's vestibular system—the part of the inner ear that maintains equilibrium—and render a victim unconscious. Researchers at the Massachusetts Institute of Technology and at American Technology Corp. of Poway, California, have developed a high-frequency beam of sound so narrow that the noise seems as though it's coming from right in front of you,

The Other Side

HUSSEIN & AL QAEDA

According to Richard Butler, who ran the U.N. arms inspection of Iraq in the late 1990s, "it would be foolish in the extreme not to assume that he [Iraqi leader Saddam Hussein] is: developing long-range missile capabilities; at work again on building nuclear weapons; and adding to the chemical and biological warfare weapons he concealed during the UNSCOM inspection period."

Butler's warning, expressed in his book *The Greatest Threat*, becomes even more chilling given reliable reports that al Qaeda is seeking similarly dangerous weapons, such as "dirty" radioactive bombs and chemical devices. CIA director George Tenet told Congress in early 2002 that "al Qaeda was working to acquire some of the most dangerous chemical agents and toxins. Documents recovered from al Qaeda facilities in Afghanistan show that [Osama] bin Laden was pursuing a sophisticated biological weapons research program."

And of course, the possibility that the two forces—Iraq and al Qaeda—are working jointly to pursue chemical, biological, or other dangerous weapons is not entirely farfetched either. In the weeks following the September 11 terrorist attacks on New York and Washington, there were reports that one of the hijackers, Mohammed Atta, had met with a high-level Iraqi intelligence official in the Czech Republic.

The religious extremists of al Qaeda and the dictator Hussein may not have much in common besides mutual enemies—but that's enough to make them both legitimate threats to the U.S.

even when it's transmitted from hundreds of yards away. The military could use this technology to temporarily deafen or confuse an adversary. Another sound alternative is a high-frequency pulse emitter, small enough to fit in a briefcase, that combatants could use to disrupt or burn out unprotected electronic circuits in computers. This could wreak havoc upon aircraft flight controls, financial networks, power grids, and other key points in a nation's infrastructure. In 2001, a congressional committee investigating the United States's vulnerability to sonic attack actually funded the development of just such a weapon.

At its research laboratory at Kirtland Air Force Base, the U.S. Air Force is studying high-powered microwave pulse weapons that would also target an enemy's electronic pressure points. A powerful, long-range microwave pulse lasting only a fraction of a second could fry the intricate guidance circuitry of an incoming guided missile. Other targets might include enemy communications equipment and battle-management computers. Microwave weapons, which could be mounted on trucks or airplanes, offer a stealthy, covert function as well. Microwaves can penetrate the seams in buildings to damage computers and radios, leaving only the slightest trace of their presence. Only close inspection of the equipment will reveal that there was an intentional microwave assault. They may also prove to be effective weapons against satellites in space, and unofficial reports suggest that developers at Kirtland have already achieved such a capability.

Here is how a microwave gun might work: An electrical pulse creates a stream of high-energy charged particles that operators accelerate into a cavity. The cavity causes the charged particles to "bunch," or accelerate coherently, which creates electromagnetic radiation in the form of microwaves. The operators then transmit these to the target using a specially designed antenna. The principal appeal of microwaves for

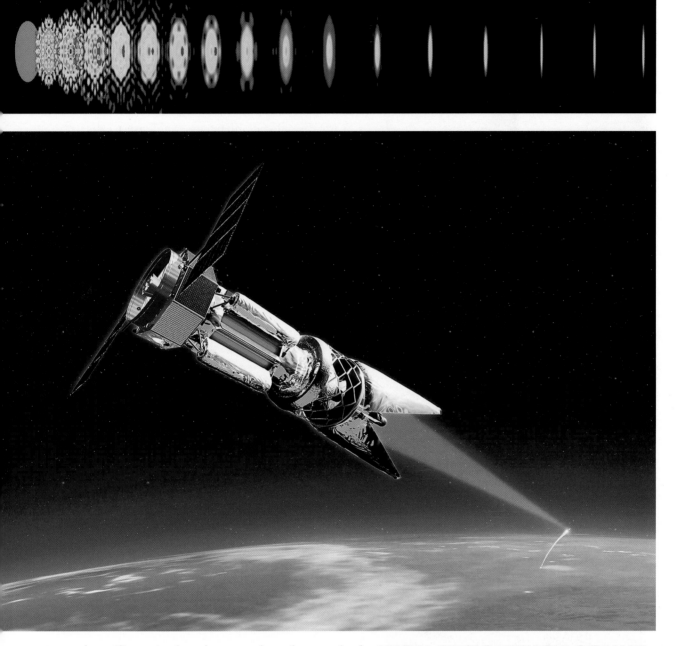

the military is that they travel at the speed of light, which would add infinite meaning to the phrase "point-and-shoot." A microwave weapon could have a firing rate of as much as 100 shots per second, and the supply of ammunition is almost inexhaustible.

Combat analysts became interested in microwave weapons after participating in war games in which a hypothetical adversary's first act was to detonate a nuclear weapon in space.

HIGH-FREQUENCY SOUND BEAM/SPACE LASER

Researchers at MIT are developing a high-frequency sound beam (top) that could be used to deafen or disorient an adversary. The U.S. Air Force has tested technology for a space-based laser (above) that could shoot down ballistic missiles and hit targets on the ground.

The explosion generated an electromagnetic pulse (EMP) that rendered GPS navigation, communications, and spy satellites—all of which are currently critical to military operations—inoperative. Needless to say, this was a eureka moment for military brass.

Microwave weapons would also generate microwave pulses. Scientists at Oak Ridge National Laboratory in Tennessee have proposed building an EMP weapon that would disrupt a human being's short-term memory and cause him or her to lose control of voluntary bodily functions. While such an attack would be very embarrassing, at least the victim would not be able to recall the humiliating episode.

Other nonlethal weapons that could cause singular damage are biological agents designed to "eat" materials such as Kevlar, metal, asphalt, cement, paints, or lubricants. The roots of this idea lie in a proposal to the Office of Naval

Spotlight

ACTIVE DENIAL TECHNOLOGY

Whenever a small group of soldiers faces a large, hostile crowd, tensions can escalate quickly. The troops can get backed into a corner and panic, or they can be forced to defend themselves. Equipped with lethal weapons, the soldiers will probably exercise lethal force if they are forced to act. In peacekeeping or humanitarian missions, these conditions often cause a downward spiral to disaster.

The U.S. military is currently developing a variety of nonlethal weapons for soldiers in these situations so that the standoffs may be resolved, if not entirely peaceably, then at least not disastrously. Among the most promising of the several alternatives is a directed energy beam that inflicts a brief, intense burning sensation on the target's skin. The weapon (left, in illustration), which would be mounted on top of a Humvee, fires bursts of electromagnetic energy that pass through clothing but penetrate the skin to a depth of only $\frac{1}{64}$th of an inch. The recipient of the electromagnetic waves would feel as though he had touched a hot light bulb.

While its range is classified, the weapon can be adjusted to heat the skin to a variety of temperatures, up to as much as 130° F. The U.S. Marine Corps, which is overseeing the $40 million program dubbed "active denial technology," says the weapon could be fielded by 2009. It could be an essential and most welcome tool in future peacekeeping missions.

MICROWAVE WEAPONS

Scientists at Kirtland Air Force Base in New Mexico use an anechoic chamber to radiate an F-16 with micro-wave energy. The specialists at Kirtland are trying to determine how well they have protected the F-16's systems against microwave energy, which military experts continue to evaluate for potential weapons applications.

Research to create genetically engineered microorganisms that would quickly corrode roads and runways, or the metal parts, coatings, and lubricants of weapons, vehicles, and support equipment. The weapon would function like a kind of accelerated case of Ebola-virus rust and could be dropped into an enemy's motor pool inside bombs or missiles.

Last but far from least are lasers, the weapons of the future that capture everyone's imagination, largely thanks to science fiction films such as the *Star Wars* series. In these movies, laser weapons of various types flash across the screen, wreaking havoc on targets. In real life, the airborne laser, an anti-missile weapon housed aboard a 747, is close to being functional, and the space-based laser is on the drawing board. The primary technological obstacle to the production of laser weapons is size. They are simply too big at the moment, and scaling them down to a manageable size is a significant engineering challenge. The Pentagon's research arm, DARPA, is developing what could be a radical solution to the problem in a high-power fiber-optic laser. Using microelectromechanical (MEMS) technology, DARPA hopes to generate a laser within the microscopic confines of a fiberoptic cable. While the laser power generated from a single fiber-optic cable would be about one kilowatt, combining the laser power of 100 or more would yield a useful weapon. With MEMS techniques and solid-state lasers, scientists could create a weapon small enough to use in vehicles, ships, and planes.

A laser weapon could be used against many targets, and it also could be a very effective counter to heat-seeking missiles, which are both dangerous and plentiful among the armies of the world. As the technology blossoms and miniaturizes, laser rifles, à la *Star Wars*, may become a reality. The advantage of portable laser weapons is obvious—laser beams travel at the speed of light, and the only constraint on ammunition for a laser rifle would be the amount of electrical power available. DARPA hopes to demonstrate a prototype of a single fiberoptic laser in 2003.

Can Luke Skywalker be far behind?

GEAR

GEAR

T O FIND OUT WHAT SORT OF GEAR the modern U.S. soldier totes into battle, read Mark Bowden's superb book *Black Hawk Down*, or rent the film of the same title. A blow-by-blow account of the ill-fated U.S. mission to capture two lieutenants of the Somali warlord Mohamed Farrah Aidid, the book is a riveting page-turner. Two American units, Delta Force and the Rangers, led the raid, which was supposed to last one hour but devolved into a ferocious 15-hour firefight after Somali warriors shot down two of the Americans' Black Hawk helicopters.

Pinned down by thousands of heavily armed Somalis, the Rangers and Delta Force fought their way out of the byzantine streets of Mogadishu, the African nation's capital. Eighteen American soldiers died and scores were wounded before Delta and the Rangers reached safe ground—but the death toll among Somalis was far greater, probably more than a thousand.

How did the U.S. forces inflict such heavy casualties despite being vastly outnumbered and tactically disadvantaged? Among the many answers to that question are superior organization, technology, and the focus of the following chapter: gear.

The U.S. soldiers wore standard desert camouflage clothing made famous during the Gulf War. The camo is constructed of rip-stop cotton, and if

LIGHT MORTAR PLATOON
Members of the United States's 15th Marine Expeditionary Unit, a light mortar platoon, tote their gear to a forward base in southern Afghanistan during the war against the Taliban and al Qaeda in November 2001.

it ever gets wet—though that wasn't likely in the desert city of Mogadishu—it dries in a few minutes. Over their torsos they wore green camo vests called Personnel Armor System, Ground Troop (PASGT). These anti-fragmentation vests are a little bulky, and particularly hot in the desert, but well worth the discomfort, since, when combined with the Interim Small Arms Protective Overvest (ISAPO), they can stop a 7.62mm round.

The *Black Hawk* soldiers wore kevlar helmets that are lighter and stronger than the old G.I. steel bucket. If they had brought along any food (they didn't, since the extraction was supposed to take only an hour), it would have come in the form of the U.S. military's Meals, Ready to Eat (MREs), which are compact and self-heating. The MREs replace the C-rations of earlier U.S. campaigns.

The most high-tech gear in the modern soldier's repertoire is his headphone communication system, which connects him to his fellow troops and back to base. In the early days of the 20th century, soldiers used carrier pigeons to get messages to and from base. These winged couriers gave way to wire telephones, which led to backpack-mounted radiophones whose operators had to stick by the commanding officer during battles. After World War II, hefty walkie-talkies replaced radiophones. The headset system is the latest unit in the communications line, but as high-tech as it is, it often gives way, during noisy combat or stealthy recon, to a primitive form of communication: hand signals.

The U.S. soldiers in the Battle of Mogadishu practiced "vertical envelopment," military-speak for placing troops in a target area from aircraft—they rappelled down ropes suspended from helicopters. In other situations, troops might parachute into an enemy field at night—in that case, they would use a compact, rectangular parachute. Highly controllable, the new parachute replaces the circular chutes of D-Day, which sometimes left a soldier thousands of meters away from his target. Once on the ground, modern U.S. troops locate each other using their portable headsets.

Ultimately, the U.S. soldier's high survival rate and extremely high kill rate can be attributed to a number of factors, but prominent among them is his state-of-the-art gear, which has been refined for decades with one goal in mind: to maximize his safety and his effectiveness.

[GEAR]
WORKHORSES

COVERING HIM FROM HEAD TO TOE, AND PROVIDING
HIS DAILY FOOD, WATER, AND SHELTER, WORKHORSE
GEAR SUPPLIES THE MODERN U.S. SOLDIER WITH
EVERYTHING HE NEEDS TO PERFORM HIS DUTIES.

COMBAT BOOTS/ DESERT CAMO

In Afghanistan, a U.S. soldier (above) uses his boots for a pillow. His helmet camouflage is identical to the camo Gen. Norman Schwarzkopf (opposite) and his charges wore during Desert Storm.

URING WORLD WAR II , U.S. forces had little besides a steel helmet to protect their bodies from the hazards of combat. When you consider that this helmet couldn't stop a direct hit from an enemy bullet, you understand how vulnerable American soldiers were on the battlefields of the most titanic conflict in history. Since bulletproof vests didn't exist, a round to the body often meant one of two things for the U.S. grunt in WWII. It was either a "million-dollar wound"—meaning the soldier was hurt enough to go home—or a fatal one.

Lightweight body armor appeared during the Korean War, greatly improving the grunt's lot and saving countless lives. One U.S. Army private in Korea saw a grenade roll into his position, and, surrounded by

PASGT HELMET/VEST

The military's new Kevlar helmet (left) offers better head coverage than its predecessor and will stop a 9-mm round. When combined with its overlay, the new armored vest (below) can stop a .30-caliber round.

most of his company, he dived on the pineapple just before it exploded. The grenade kicked him up in the air a few feet, but because he was wearing body armor he suffered little more than a severely bruised chest. In another incident, a U.S. Marine was on patrol when a mortar shell landed about 10 feet from him. He picked the shell fragments out of his torso and went on his merry way. One of his buddies on the same patrol took six rounds to the chest from an enemy burp gun, and thanks to his body armor, all he had to show for it were a few bruises.

The new wonder substance protecting these Korean War soldiers was a combination of fiberglass cloth and plastic, named Doron, after Brig. Gen. Georges Doriot, who was chief of the research and development branch of the Army in the 1940s and '50s. Charged with developing body armor during World War II, Doriot's office produced an armored vest in time for the Korean War. Since then, body armor has been a staple of the U.S. military.

Today's vests, which the Army and the Marines have used since the early 1980s, are called Personnel Armor System, Ground Troop (PASGT). They weigh 17 pounds and provide protection against fragments. Augmented with the Interim Small Arms Protective Overvest (ISAPO), they will halt a .30-caliber round. The two vests weigh a whopping 25.1 pounds combined, a pretty hefty load for a soldier in the field, not to mention a toasty one for a guy stationed in a warm climate. But of course, most soldiers prefer stifling heat to a gaping chest wound.

The old familiar U.S. M-1 steel pot helmet, which doubled as a cooking pot for many a G.I. during World War II, has given way to the

BODY ARMOR

During war games at the U.S. Army's National Training Center at Fort Irwin, California, Sgt. Scott Decker models the latest in military gear, including the PASGT armored vest and its Interim Small Arms Protective Overvest.

PASGT Kevlar helmet. Critics say the Kevlar headgear too closely resembles Nazi Germany's M-35 helmet from World War II. Frankly, it does—and you can't cook a meal in it. But unlike the M-1, the Kevlar helmet can stop a direct hit from a 9-millimeter round, and that extra protection comes without too much extra weight. The steel-pot helmet weighed 2.3 pounds, and the Kevlar model checks in at slightly more than 3 pounds. While the World War II-era helmet came with an olive drab paint job and netting into which G.I.s could stick leaves and branches for camouflage, the Kevlar is covered with camouflage cloth material.

A similar material covers today's combat soldier from head to toe. The military likes to refer to camouflage uniforms as BDUs, which stands for Battle Dress Uniforms. BDUs come in almost as many patterns as there are terrains. Chief among them—or at least most popular with Army brass—is the regular three-color green BDU that soldiers commonly wear in training camps and on domestic bases. But

Spotlight   MEALS READY TO EAT

A most unlikely icon of American culture, the C-Ration provided the daily bread for grunts during World War II. Short for Ration, Combat, Individual, C-Rations came in golden, dogfood-size cans. Rumor had it that they tasted like dogfood too. They quickly became famous on the homefront for their extreme austerity. C-Rations contained such comestible delicacies as meat and hash, meat and beans, and meat and vegetable stew.

During the Vietnam War, the military supplemented or replaced C-Rations with the Meal, Combat, Individual (MCI), which included 12 different menus for the infantryman's consumption. Each ration contained one canned meat item, one canned fruit item, and bread or a dessert selection. "Although the meat item can be eaten cold, it is more palatable when heated," read the official quartermaster's report, without intentional irony. But palatability, of course, was not the military's goal—calories were. Each MCI packed 1,200 calories, providing the grunt with 3,600 a day.

The meager silver lining inside this culinary dark cloud was that each ration came with an accessory pack containing a spoon, instant coffee, creamer, sugar, salt, chewing gum, toilet paper, and even a pack of cigarettes and a book of matches. Yet despite the presence of MCIs, World War II-era C-Rations remained in circulation well into the 1970s.

In the early 1980s, military cooks stirred up Meals, Ready to Eat, or MREs (left), which remain the workhorse form of sustenance for U.S. soldiers. Each 1,200-calorie MRE contains an entrée, crackers, cheese or peanut butter spread, dessert, a beverage, a spoon, and a flameless exothermic ration heater. MREs come in boxes of 12 meals, which fit into four bags of three meals each. The military says they are tasty, and to hungry soldiers they probably are. The military also encourages soldiers to save the empty boxes—they can be filled with sand, snow, ice, or dirt and then stacked like bricks to take the place of sandbags as fortifications in the field. Even good old C-Rations couldn't do that.

before hitting the sands of Saudi Arabia for Operation Desert Shield, U.S. troops donned the now-famous three-color desert BDU. Forces battling the Taliban and al Qaeda in Afghanistan wear a six-color desert camo, unless they are members of the 10th Mountain Division, who wear white camo for the snowy terrain. For action in subtropical climates, U.S. troops wear the tiger-stripe pattern that clothed Special Forces in Vietnam.

All U.S. BDUs except the tiger-stripe are composed of rip-stop cotton, and all of them dry within minutes after getting wet. The pants come with huge side cargo pockets for carrying any additional equipment a soldier needs at his

AN/PVS-7 GOGGLES

A U.S. soldier demonstrates the military's night-vision goggles, which can come equipped with high-magnification lenses, a compass, an infrared spotlight lens, and a bracket for mounting them on a helmet.

fingertips, and they all have button flys, which, unlike zippers, won't get stuck in rainy, sandy, muddy, or frigid combat theaters. Small straps on both sides of the waist make the pants adjustable so that a few sizes fit all, and there are straps sewn into the cuffs to draw together the pant leg and tuck it into a combat boot. The boots generally come in black or desert sand colors.

RA-3185 MIR /RA-108/HEADSETS

Depending on the combat situation, U.S. soldiers have their choice of three headsets for communicating with their fellow platoon members: the RA-3185 Modular Infantry Radio (above left), which has a noise-canceling boom microphone and an adjustable earpiece; the RA-108 (above right); and the RA-315 Integrated Helmet System, both of which come equipped with Active Noise Reduction (ANR) and can function in noisy armored vehicles.

For nighttime combat or observation, U.S. troops carry AN/PVS-7 night-vision goggles. The goggles have two eyepieces, like glasses or divers' goggles, but a single lens illuminates the entire field of vision. The manufacturer boasts that a soldier can make all necessary adjustments to the goggles with one hand. Each pair of AN/PVS-7s comes with a military head strap and several options, including high-magnification lenses, a compass, an infrared spotlight lens, and a helmet-mounting bracket.

While the AN/PVS-7 enables the modern U.S. soldier to see at night, the RA-3185 Cobra Modular Infantry Radio headset allows him to communicate with his fellow infantry in most combat situations. This nifty device looks like the hands-free microphone that Madonna wears during her concerts. The Cobra has a noise-canceling boom microphone that the soldier positions in front of his mouth, and a single earpiece that's adjustable and stands a short distance from the ear for comfort and to allow the soldier

to hear surrounding noise with both ears. Depending on his preference, a soldier can affix the device with a headband, helmet clips, or headstraps.

Two headset models come with active noise reduction (ANR) for use in noisy armored vehicles. The RA-108 Headset is for mechanized infantry, and the RA-315 Integrated Helmet System is for troops in tanks and other fighting vehicles. Invented by the stereo manufacturer Bose in the 1980s, ANR allows armored crews to communicate without shouting. All of these headsets are sleek enough to fit underneath the soldier's helmet.

Not particularly sleek, but surprisingly lightweight, is the U.S. soldier's ALICE pack, or All-purpose Lightweight Individual Carrying Equipment pack. (Can't you just see Army brass staying up all night thinking of that one?) It comes in one color, olive drab, and it's huge: In its frame, the ALICE pack is wider than the soldier and nearly as tall. The typical unmodified

CANTEEN

It may be the soldier's simplest piece of gear, but it's also one of his most important: The military's current canteen is made of sturdy green plastic and comes with a filter that removes bugs, bacteria, and chemicals.

pack contains one large storage area for the items a soldier can't live without during a few months' deployment. These include a tent, a sleeping bag, mosquito netting, extra clothing, and a spare pair of boots, to name a few. The ALICE has six pouches in the front for toting night-vision goggles, headphones, letters from home, or the modern soldier's food rations, Meals Ready to Eat (MREs).

Filled to capacity, the ALICE pack should weigh 100 pounds, though you can rest assured that most soldiers can stuff them till they're heavier than that. Soldiers typically camouflage their packs with a special cover of military camo colors and waterproof them with a spray-on product.

The last, but far from least, piece of gear the well-equipped soldier packs is a canteen. Whereas earlier canteens consisted of two pieces of aluminum, today's one-quart units are made of hard green plastic and come with a filter that removes bugs, bacteria, chemicals, and

Inventor

KEVLAR

Fortune magazine dubbed it "a miracle in search of a market" during its 15-year developmental stage, but Kevlar, the brand name for the Dupont company's exceptionally strong aramid fiber, has proved worth the wait. Scientists at Dupont had been struggling for years to develop a stronger and more durable nylon-related fiber when chemist Stephanie L. Klowek created the first liquid crystal polymer in 1965. Klowek's polymer could be cold spun, and it provided the basis for what we know today as Kevlar, a fiber that is five times stronger than steel.

Dupont spent $500 million developing its "miracle," which ended up finding several markets and easily paying back its development cost. Manufacturers of cut-resistant gloves, tires, and, of course, lightweight body armor rely on Kevlar for their products. All of the U.S. military's state-of-the-art combat helmets are made of Kevlar. They weigh only three pounds and provide U.S. soldiers with unprecedented protection. Police departments the world over use Kevlar vests and helmets. The standard for high-performance body armor, some forms of Kevlar can stop direct hits from 9-millimeter and .30-caliber rounds. The fiber has saved the lives of more than 2,500 officers.

Klowek, who earned her chemistry degree from what is now Carnegie Mellon University, joined Dupont in 1946. In 1950, she began her search for the new polymers and lower-temperature condensation processes required to create specialty textile fibers. She hit upon her liquid crystal polymer 15 years later, and in 1981, Kevlar was ready for the market. Klowek won the National Medal of Technology in 1996.

pesticides. That filter is a welcome addition for the thirsty fighting man in the field and further proof of the U.S. military's commitment to improve even the simplest pieces of gear in its ranks in the 21st century. But the canteens still come encased in an olive-green cover. Some things will never change.

READY FOR DUTY

FROM THE SOPHISTICATED LAND WARRIOR SYSTEM TO THE UTILITARIAN PARATROOPER MOUNTAIN BIKE, THE MILITARY'S READY-FOR-DUTY GEAR GIVES U.S. SOLDIERS THE EDGE IN ALMOST ANY COMBAT SITUATION.

TRUSTING IN THEIR COVER OF DARKNESS, a band of warriors treks through the desert landscape believing they are invisible to enemy eyes. Ten miles away, perched atop a small hill, a U.S. soldier scans the terrain with a binocular-style night-vision system. He quickly spots the night trekkers but is not sure what to make of them at first, as the men wear civilian clothes. The American refocuses, and his night-vision system, produced by the Photonics Division of Intevac in Santa Clara, California, provide enough resolution for him to discern the telltale shapes of AK-47 rifles and rocket-propelled grenade launchers slung over the shoulders of the men walking in the distant darkness.

The night-vision system registers the image by sending a series of

LAND WARRIOR/ MAV

Sgt. Scott Decker (opposite) demonstrates a prototype of the Army's Land Warrior fighting system, which will include a video camera, computer, and laser rangefinder. Micro Air Vehicles, or MAVs (above), will be key recon tools in the 21st century.

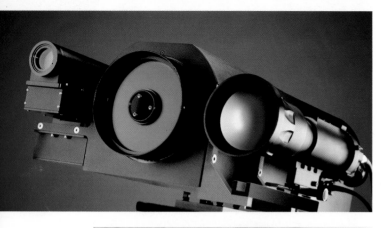

NIGHT-VISION SYSTEM

Using laser pulses, the military's long-range night-vision system (left) can generate an image of an enemy in darkness up to 10 miles away, allowing U.S. soldiers to get the drop on him.

JOINT TACTICAL RADIO SYSTEM (JTRS)

Soon, all branches of the military will have radio headsets (left) that comply with JTRS technology, easing communication among the branches during chaotic combat situations.

OPTICAL SIGHT

Land Warrior soldiers' rifles come equipped with an optical sight (right) that has a range of 300 meters and is capable of relaying the image it captures in its crosshairs across a network.

undetectable 1.5-micron laser pulses toward the target. A camera inside the night-vision system constructs a still video image of the enemy figures out of the individual photons of light bouncing off them. Using his GPS-equipped radio, the U.S. soldier quickly transmits the position of the enemy soldiers to an AC-130 gunship flying on patrol. Within minutes, the plane arrives to dispatch the night-stalking desert group. At dawn, the U.S. soldier will

hike out with his squad to examine the bodies and gather any available intelligence.

Long-range night-vision systems are among the many items becoming available to U.S. soldiers as they march into the digital age. Another key piece of gear is the radio, which takes on increasing importance as the Army, Air Force, Navy, and Marines forge more and more joint operations. During the U.N. peacekeeping mission to Somalia in 1993, for example, U.S.

ground and air forces were unable to communicate directly because they used radios with different frequencies. Somali warriors killed 18 U.S. soldiers and wounded dozens of others during the chaotic Battle of Mogadishu, and it's entirely possible that improved communication among the U.S. forces might have averted or minimized the losses. Enter the Joint Tactical Radio System (JTRS), which uses "software radio" to address the problem of communication between the military branches during combat. Whereas the old radio is hardwired to accept a limited number of frequencies, software radio uses a computer to translate all incoming signals into digital form, then decodes them into audible messages. Soldiers can then recode and retransmit those messages on any frequency they desire. Software radio thus makes it a simple matter for a message to travel from headquarters to a Navy helicopter to Army Rangers on the ground.

In Action

MICRO AIR VEHICLES

While the combat mission most often cited for micro air vehicles is so-called over-the-hilll reconnaissance, the mini unmanned aerial vehicles could be deployed for a variety of other purposes, including urban warfare operations, biochemical detection missions, and search-and-rescue operations.

In an urban theater of war, U.S. soldiers could send small, coordinated groups of MAVs several kilometers ahead of their position to survey an inner-city sector and relay observations back to the squad. The extremely agile MAVs will be able to negotiate the complex and tight spaces of a city and even "see" through windows to monitor enemy activity.

MAVs are small enough to avoid detection by the enemy, and they could be equipped to place sensors atop enemy vehicles for tracking or to detect biochemical agents. And in the not-too-distant future, MAVs may be able to penetrate interior spaces in cities and conduct missions inside enemy strongholds.

From a safe distance, the squad members will be able to monitor all of the MAVs' work on their visor displays and plan their next move accordingly. It sounds like science fiction, but the MAV is already a reality.

PARATROOPER MOUNTAIN BIKE

Rugged, lightweight, and compact enough to fit in a 3-by-3-foot shoulder bag, the military's new mountain bike gets its name from its ability to withstand being dropped by parachute from a plane. Its frame is made of lightweight aluminum but has steel supports in the rear to accommodate a rider wearing a pack.

All branches of the service are adopting a more computerized, network-centric approach to warfare, and the greatest difficulty they all face is applying this approach to the individual soldier in the field. Chief among the several problems in this regard is the size and weight of the power source that the soldier must carry. No one expects him to lug a laptop and a bulky battery pack into battle. The Army is developing a solution in a program called Land Warrior, scheduled for implementation in 2004. Land Warrior will outfit every soldier with lightweight, computer-operated gear that, among other features, will allow him to stay in constant contact with every other member of his platoon.

The Land Warrior program will include a helmet-mounted video display, a rifle with either a video or thermal sight, a radio with a built-in

GPS receiver, two computers, and two thin-film batteries to power everything for up to 12 hours. Each of the two computers is about the size of a videotape, with commercial, off-the-shelf microprocessors. This makes them relatively inexpensive and easy to upgrade as technology improves.

Like modern-day corporate workers, Land Warrior soldiers will carry a Local Area Network (LAN) card in lieu of a bulky radio. The LAN card sends encrypted voice and data transmissions over a 2-kilometer range. It also conserves power by cycling on and off every 10 milliseconds. In another energy-conservation feature, the computers determine the amount of signal strength required for each communication and parcel it out accordingly.

The Land Warrior program will also equip each soldier's M-4 rifle with an optical sight, which, in addition to having a range of 300 meters, doubles as a communications tool. When a squad leader moves forward to reconnoiter, he will be able to aim his M-4 and relay the image in its sights back to the rest of the platoon. This means the squad leader doesn't have to risk exposing himself to hostile fire by returning to

MOLLE PACK

The MOLLE pack comes with a contoured plastic frame and can haul 25 pieces of equipment, 180 rounds of ammunition, two hand grenades, and two canteens. Soldiers can add up to 18 pouches to the central rucksack.

brief the platoon on the results of his reconnaissance; the platoon members will see exactly what he sees on their headset displays. Each soldier can also point a gun-mounted laser at a target and feed the targeting data directly into the network, eliminating the need for voice transmission of coordinates to call in artillery fire, for example.

The military will add these new capabilities without increasing the 90 pounds of gear each soldier currently carries into battle. Software and electronic equipment will only get lighter as technology improves. New materials shaved 10 pounds off the weight of body armor, for instance, while making it more resistant to enemy fire. In addition to shrapnel, the armor can now stop a round from an AK-47.

The Land Warrior program includes a Kevlar helmet that is cut a little shorter than the current model, making it more comfortable to wear, and knee and elbow guards for protection in rugged terrain. The Army plans to produce 64,000 Land Warrior systems at a cost of $6 billion.

A less costly development, and one that will also reduce the dangers of reconnaissance, is the military's development of mini unmanned aerial vehicles. Like much of the Land Warrior program, these will depend on networked communication. The first of them, Dragon Eye, is portable—it fits in a backpack—and snaps together like a model plane. Equipped with a video camera, a GPS receiver, an infrared sensor, and a radio transmitter, Dragon Eye can buzz over the next hill and take a look for the platoon. A soldier will launch Dragon Eye, which has a wingspan of 48 inches, with a bungee cord, and recover it with a simple belly-mounted parachute. As electronics systems continue to shrink, micro air vehicles, like AeroVironment's Black Widow, may also see field use. Soldiers would hand-launch these mini aircraft, which are only 6 inches in diameter, like paper airplanes and view the images they transmit through video goggles. Some of these micro air vehicles may ultimately assume the shape and flight patterns of insects, a configuration that may offer better maneuverability and stealth.

But not all of the new gear is as high-tech as an insect-like micro air vehicle. Some of it is simply a new take on an old standby. U.S. Special Forces in Afghanistan participated in the first cavalry charge of the 21st century, and they may yet storm to the front lines on bicycles. A mountain bike is particularly suited to the rugged terrain of a country like Afghanistan, and DARPA, the Pentagon's research arm, has developed one for military use. Dubbed the Paratrooper, the bike folds into a compact, 3-by-3-foot package and can fit into a shoulder bag. The frame is a mix of lightweight aluminum with steel supports in the rear to bear the extra weight of a rider carrying a pack. That pack is a redesigned, modular piece of equipment. It's called MOLLE (for Modular Lightweight Load-carrying Equipment), and it features a contoured plastic frame, with a central rucksack capable of supporting 18 additional pouches of various sizes.

Sporting their wide array of new gear, 21st century U.S. soldiers will take the field with every technological advantage. But gear, of course, only goes so far: Coordination, commitment, and courage will finish the job.

Spotlight HARDSUIT 2000

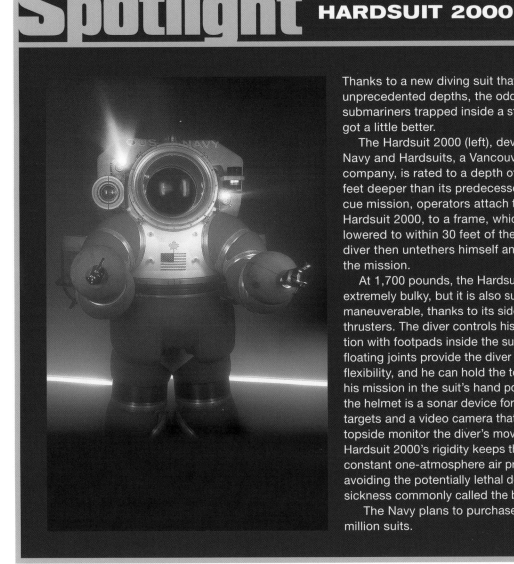

Thanks to a new diving suit that can plunge to unprecedented depths, the odds of rescuing submariners trapped inside a stricken boat just got a little better.

The Hardsuit 2000 (left), developed by the Navy and Hardsuits, a Vancouver, B.C.-based company, is rated to a depth of 2,000 feet, 800 feet deeper than its predecessor. During a rescue mission, operators attach the diver, in the Hardsuit 2000, to a frame, which is then lowered to within 30 feet of the target. The diver then untethers himself and proceeds with the mission.

At 1,700 pounds, the Hardsuit 2000 is extremely bulky, but it is also surprisingly maneuverable, thanks to its side-mounted thrusters. The diver controls his pitch and direction with footpads inside the suit. Oil-filled floating joints provide the diver with arm and leg flexibility, and he can hold the tools required for his mission in the suit's hand pods. Attached to the helmet is a sonar device for finding hidden targets and a video camera that lets colleagues topside monitor the diver's movements. The Hardsuit 2000's rigidity keeps the diver's body in constant one-atmosphere air pressure, thereby avoiding the potentially lethal decompression sickness commonly called the bends.

The Navy plans to purchase four of the $2.7 million suits.

CUTTING EDGE

THE CUTTING-EDGE MILITARY GEAR CURRENTLY ON THE DRAWING BOARD IN LABS AROUND THE COUNTRY MAY SEEM LIKE SCIENCE FICTION, BUT MUCH OF IT COULD BE REALITY BY THE END OF THE DECADE.

IT'S THE YEAR 2025, and squads of helmeted, black-clad U.S. soldiers are picking their way through the streets of a hostile city. Without warning, a sharp report from the rifle of an enemy sniper echoes down the block. "Man down!" comes the cry, and soldiers turn with dread to see one of their own lying in the street. But they soon discover that the soldier is only stunned. His body armor—made of composite materials woven with carbon nanotubes, or microfibers, stronger than steel—has stopped the small-caliber round.

Almost immediately, medics at headquarters confirm that the soldier is OK. The inside layer of his uniform is composed of a network of microprocessors that monitor his skin and body. All of the soldiers in

OFW/ FUTURE WARRIOR

The Army hopes to have its Objective Force Warrior (opposite)–which is a precursor prototype to the Future Warrior 2025 (above)–in the field by 2010. The system includes physiological sensors and full body armor.

action wear this uniform, which continually transmits life-support data to the command post over a wireless network. The medics can see that while the downed soldier's heart rate and stress level are up, he does not have a life-threatening injury. He is working up quite a sweat, though, so the portable air conditioner on his belt kicks in, circulating coolant in threadlike tubes that run the length and width of his uniform.

"Have a drink of water," the medics tell him, and he hears the message as if it were a thought in his mind: He has a receiver in his helmet that conducts sound through the bones of his head. This system allows soldiers to communicate during combat without giving away their positions. The soldier sips from a tube inside his helmet that is connected to a water pack on his back, then he climbs to his feet and flashes the OK sign to his buddies. They don't have to be looking his way to see the gesture. The fingertips on the soldier's glove contain sensors, and the microprocessors embedded in his helmet recognize the hand sign and transmit the signal to the display inside each of the other soldiers' visors.

This is the kind of scenario envisioned by scientists working at facilities such as the U.S. Army's Soldier Systems Center (SSC) in Natick, Massachusetts. For these specialists, the future is as much about keeping U.S. soldiers alive as it is about doing the opposite for enemy troops. They've compiled some of their ideas about the future of warfare in a notional program called Future Warrior 2025, which would be the military's next step after Land Warrior, set to debut in 2004. Initially, the Future Warrior concept

FUTURE WARRIOR 2025

The soldier of the future (left) would wear sleek body armor, sport a helmet with a video camera and a display, and tote a four-barrel firearm with a choice of ammo (above). His suit would include a power conduit (above right).

involved a 5-pound weapons pod strapped to the soldier's wrist, but the SSC has since scrapped that idea in favor of a handheld firearm with similar capabilities. But most of the program's ideas involve systems that monitor the soldier's health and keep him in constant communication with other soldiers and mission control. The scientists also envision soldiers packing a portable power system to make it all possible.

Each future warrior would wear a motorcycle-style helmet embedded with numerous microprocessors that would control all of the subsystems involved in this outfit. The microprocessors would be able to warp images transmitted from headquarters to match the curvature of the helmet's visor, so the visor would double as a display. Soldiers could control their weapons with voice-activated software that recognizes only the vocal patterns of the weapon's owner. If the weapon fell into the hands of the enemy, he wouldn't be able to use it. (On the other hand, neither would a soldier's fellow squad member, if it came to that.)

While the helmet might compromise the soldier's field of vision slightly, it would contain eight microphones to give him 360-degree

enhanced hearing. It would also contain a digital camera that would provide both visible and infrared video images. Other electronic components would supply imaging links to headquarters and might also allow the soldier to remotely control miniature spy planes.

The future warrior's uniform may be black to start with, but it wouldn't have to stay that way. A new method of weaving promises to yield uniforms that can change color, chameleon-style, to provide camouflage in any environment. In this method, electrically charged polymer drops produce a dense web of form-fitting fibers. By adding electrophoretic inks to the mix, the Army could create a uniform that would change color in response to different types of light, making a soldier practically invisible in any situation. The uniform fabrics of the future may also contain enzymes and other catalysts that would break down toxic substances to provide protection against biological or chemical agents.

Clearly, the 21st century soldier's uniform will be a far cry from the heavy cotton twill getups of World War II soldiers, and even from the desert camo that outfitted U.S. soldiers in the Gulf War and Afghanistan. It will probably have three layers: The outer skin will consist of flexible composite material formed by carbon nanotubes; the middle layer will be a series of lightweight, ballistic-resistant ceramic plates covering vital body areas; and the inner layer will be the aforemen-

POWER SOURCE

The crucial element of all warrior-of-the-future scenarios is power and how to extend the system's energy supply. The Army's Objective Force Warrior program hopes to pair a hybrid fuel cell with advanced rechargeable batteries (left) to provide power for 72 hours.

OBJECTIVE FORCE WARRIOR

A U.S. soldier (right) demonstrates the Army's original Objective Force Warrior system prototype, which included a rifle-mounted video camera, sophisticated communications technology, and body armor.

Conception

FUTURE WARRIOR

Leading the way in the U.S. Army's ongoing effort to upgrade the capabilities of its individual soldiers is the U.S. Army Soldier Systems Center (SSC) in Natick, Massachusetts. The SSC is instrumental in coordinating research, allocating funding, and attracting the best ideas, some of which may come from companies that never have worked on government projects before. "There is an awful lot of great technology being developed out there," says Pete Wallace, a project engineer with the Objective Force Warrior (OFW) program. "The question is how to tap into those sources that for one reason or another stay away from government contracting."

To do that, the SSC has unveiled a new contracting approach that cuts red tape and makes it easier for companies to do business with the government. The Army doesn't want bureaucracy to block access to a vital resource. Indeed, the OFW program, which launched in October 2001, will feature up to four competing industrial teams developing concepts for a warrior of the future, and the Army offers incentives for traditional government contractors to include new sources in their approach.

tioned microprocessors that monitor life signs and provide a power conduit for all of the necessary electronics. Liquid-hydrogen-fueled microturbines will supply the power—a steady stream of 2 watts of electricity, with surges of up to 20 watts. A replaceable, plug-in cartridge will provide enough power for six days in the field.

All of these systems will be as lightweight as technology will allow. Taken together—and this includes the 5-pound weapon and the 5-pound air conditioner each soldier will wear on his hip—the entire set of subsystems would weigh about 30 pounds. Today's soldiers typically haul about 90 pounds of gear for a three-day mission.

The future warrior's systems depend on what are now nascent technologies, still in the drawing-board phase in laboratories across the country. Among them are micromechanical systems that combine computers with tiny mechanical devices, and nanotechnology that dramatically reduces the size of powerful electronic components. Also crucial to the development of these systems are carbon nanotubes, discovered in 1991, which can be woven into everyday fabrics. In addition to their stronger-than-Superman attributes, carbon nanotubes may provide protection against laser weapons of the future, since they can absorb a laser's energy and then return to their original state.

Surprisingly, soldiers may not have to wait until 2025 to reap the benefits of the Future Warrior concepts. The Army is so enamored of these ideas that it has launched a new program called Objective Force Warrior. The aim is to turn as many of the Future Warrior concepts as possible into working systems by 2010. To that end, Objective Force is pursuing different technologies from the ones the scientists at SSC are using. One of them will be a hybrid fuel cell paired with advanced rechargeable batteries to supply a soldier's power needs for 72 hours.

A shorter-term goal at the SSC is to reduce the weight of a soldier's gear from the current 90 pounds to about 45 pounds, roughly the weight carried by warriors in Roman times. "We want a lightweight, mobile capability so that soldiers won't toss everything away except for their weapon, ammunition, and helmet when it's time to fight," says John Munroe, chairman of the program in Natick. But again, as everyone involved is keenly aware, power supply is the key. Unless it can be extended, the 21st century soldier will become the technological equivalent of a World War II-era grunt in any mission lasting longer than three days.

Still, the attraction of the new technologies and their enormous potential benefits are hard to resist. Consider a hypothetical letter, developed by an Army research panel, from a soldier to his

Spotlight EXOSKELETON

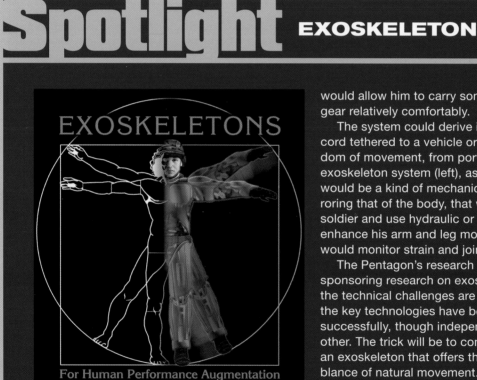

EXOSKELETONS

For Human Performance Augmentation

While some researchers work to develop materials that will lighten the soldier's load, others are taking the reverse approach, developing technology that would enable the infantryman to carry more weight. One such approach is an exoskeleton for the soldier's arms, legs, and torso that would allow him to carry some 150 pounds of gear relatively comfortably.

The system could derive its power from a cord tethered to a vehicle or a plane, or, for freedom of movement, from portable fuel cells. The exoskeleton system (left), as its name suggests, would be a kind of mechanical framework, mirroring that of the body, that would fit over the soldier and use hydraulic or electric actuators to enhance his arm and leg movements. Sensors would monitor strain and joint movements.

The Pentagon's research arm, DARPA, is sponsoring research on exoskeletons, and while the technical challenges are daunting, most of the key technologies have been demonstrated successfully, though independently of each other. The trick will be to combine them to create an exoskeleton that offers the wearer a semblance of natural movement.

And of course, an exoskeleton could be useful in non-military settings as a means to extra strength. Its developers' initial aim is to enhance a soldier's capability, but the exoskeleton will eventually wind up in the hands—or, more accurately, around the bodies—of civilians, such as firemen and rescue workers, for use in emergency operations.

OBJECTIVE FORCE WARRIOR II

The Army's current Objective Force Warrior prototype (right) features ballistic-resistant armor plates, networked communications systems, and onboard power sources.

parents dated October 30, 2017. "My suit can stop a rifle bullet. It is made of a material as flexible as my football jersey but gets hard as steel when a bullet or a knife is pushed against it. The material has some kind of chemical in it that lets fresh air pass through but stops and destroys chemical warfare agents. If I do get injured, the suit automatically inflates over the wound, stopping the bleeding and applying medicine to the injury until our medic can come help me."

Another possible supplement to such a uniform might be lightweight armor that is as flexible as cloth but can turn into a plaster cast if the wearer breaks a bone. The same material might also be used to design a forearm glove used to deliver deadly karate blows. Conversely, body armor might ultimately resemble medieval chain mail but be composed of nano-sized materials. The possibilities are almost limitless.

With a $50 million grant from the Army to jump-start research, the Massachusetts Institute of Technology created an Institute for Soldier Nanotechnologies in 2002. Among the ideas researchers there are exploring are spring-loaded combat boots that would allow a soldier to jump over a 20-foot wall. Another idea, borrowed from the science-fiction novel and film *Dune*, is to recover and distill a soldier's sweat to use as drinking water.

To paraphrase DC Comics, the soldier of the future may be able to leap tall buildings in a single bound and repel, if not outrun, a speeding bullet. And his uniform alone may earn him the nickname the Man of Steel.

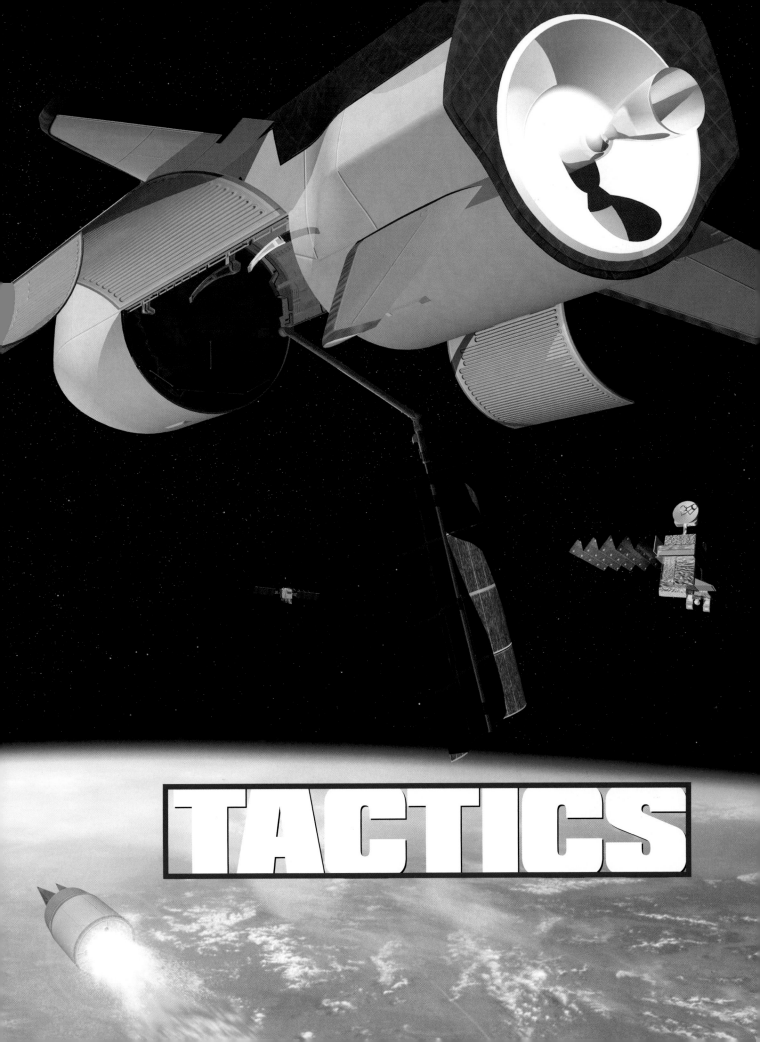

TACTICS

TACTICS

CONFEDERATE CAVALRY GENERAL Nathan Bedford Forrest summed up military tactics with a single terse sentence: "Get there first with the most men."

The early stages of the Vietnam War perfectly exemplified that strategy. Battles of attrition fought mainly on the ground of our allies, the South Vietnamese, these exchanges usually went to the force that arrived first with the most firepower. This was usually the United States, which, maddeningly, tended to then move on and leave the hard-won ground to North Vietnam.

In 1965, North Vietnamese leader Ho Chi Minh ordered a change in strategy: Vietcong troops (with a main base along the Cambodian border) would fight conventional battles only when they had a clear numerical superiority. Otherwise, they would use guerrilla tactics. The Vietcong began ambushing U.S. patrols with hit-and-run tactics. From unexploded U.S. ordnance they constructed cunningly hidden booby traps. They lived in extensive networks of tunnels that were invisible to U.S. spotter planes.

Casting about for a response, the U.S. ruled out bombing the Vietcong's supply lines, because their supplies came from the Soviet Union—one country America didn't want to tangle with. And North Vietnam's main supply route to the South, the Ho Chi Minh Trail, was very well protected.

Ho Chi Minh's shift in tactics served the Vietcong well. They began to seize the initiative in the conflict. Their network of tunnels stretched like an octopus beneath the entire nation, north and south. During the Tet Offensive in 1968, Vietcong soldiers emerged from underground near Saigon and attacked the city in force. The U.S. won the battle for Saigon, but the Vietcong surge was a sign that America couldn't win the war. So began the process toward the Paris Peace Accords, which dragged on for years. Ultimately, the U.S. pulled out, leaving South Vietnam to fall in 1975.

But the U.S. learned its painful lesson well. For this and other reasons, the Persian Gulf War 16 years later could scarcely have been more different from Vietnam. Whereas U.S. soldiers in Vietnam were mostly draftees, the forces in the Gulf were a highly motivated, all-volunteer group. Unlike in Vietnam—where North Vietnamese pilots flew Soviet-supplied fighters, and Vietcong ground forces used Soviet surface-to-air missiles against our aircraft—coalition forces quickly gained air

FRANKS/
RUMSFELD

Gen. Tommy Franks (far left), commander-in-chief of the U.S. Central Command, watches as Secretary of Defense Donald Rumsfeld briefs Pentagon reporters on military operations in Afghanistan on November 8, 2001.

Arabia. The coalition troops tore into their unmotivated, conscripted counterparts, who quickly retreated or surrendered en masse. The ground war ended after 100 hours.

As the 21st century dawned, the U.S. was engaged in military action in Afghanistan, which combines the rugged, desert terrain of Iraq with the guerrilla fighting of Vietnam. This theater could be typical of future combat scenarios, as could so-called asymmetrical warfare, which involves random, unpredictable acts of terrorism, such as the attacks on the World Trade Center and the Pentagon on September 11, 2001, and suicide bombings around the world.

In Afghanistan, as in Vietnam, the U.S. is present ostensibly as an advisor while the nation's tribal factions repel al Qaeda operatives and Taliban holdouts. It looks as though the Afghanis will win, and rule their country for the first time since the late 1970s. But as history has taught us, anything can happen in warfare—especially in our shrinking but increasingly complex world.

superiority in the Gulf War. Stealth fighters wielded highly accurate smart bombs against Iraqi radar, missile sites, and command positions. The U.S. ruled the air, and Saddam Hussein's generals were blinded, the links in their chain of command broken. Then came the ground war. As it did before the Normandy Invasion on June 6, 1944, the U.S. employed a misdirection tactic. Decoy coalition forces gathered in Kuwait, while the real invaders launched their attack on Iraq from Saudi

WORKHORSES

THE U.S. MILITARY IS TRANSFORMING ITS WORKHORSE TACTICS TO MEET THE DEMANDS OF 21ST CENTURY THEATERS, WHICH WILL REPLACE TRADITIONAL BATTLE-FIELDS WITH THE ASYMMETRY OF TERRORISM.

THE TERRORIST ATTACK THAT DESTROYED New York City's World Trade Center towers and damaged the Pentagon in Washington, D.C., on September 11, 2001, may be the watershed event that will dominate the thinking of military strategists for years to come. That attack is the most potent example so far of the threats that the United States and its principal allies will face in the 21st century. There have been others—the October 1999 attack on the USS *Cole* while it anchored in Yemen, and assaults against American embassies abroad during the '90s—but none was on U.S. soil, and none was as deadly as the September 11 atrocity. The U.S. military has dubbed this 21st century terrorism "asymmetric warfare," because it can occur almost anywhere at any time, and its perpetra-

DESERT STORM

A U.S. soldier (opposite) wears a gas mask during a chemical warfare training exercise prior to Operation Desert Storm, the U.S.-led effort (above) to repel the Iraqi army from Kuwait.

tors are scattered across the globe in terrorist cells. But whatever they call it, the military brass is just beginning to come to grips with this threat.

Before the September 11 attacks, mainstream U.S. military thinking was locked in a Cold War mode. Battle plans hinged on a war fought against a professional standing army using accepted tools of the trade—guns, tanks, and planes—supplemented by high-tech weapons, such as cruise missiles that hit targets from a

great distance. And the U.S. battle plan was tremendously effective in the Persian Gulf War, in which the combatants faced each other across the desert after a massive buildup of forces.

If the Persian Gulf War resembled a deadly game of chess, with both sides maneuvering set pieces of armor, then the U.S.'s overwhelming success in that conflict forced current and future adversaries to move off the board entirely. New adversaries will bypass military confrontation

ANTI-TERROR TACTICS

A U.S. sky marshal (left) wields a knife during a simulated hijacking at the FAA training facility in Pomona, N.J. The German federal police released wanted posters (above) for associates of the September 11 terrorists.

enemy hackers can launch attacks on the computer-dependent electrical, financial, and medical infrastructure of the U.S.

Military experts continue to debate the best ways to meet the challenges of asymmetric warfare, but one premise they agree on is the emerging "preemptive strike" doctrine. That is, the brass unanimously believes that the U.S. must have the ability to launch a preemptive strike against terrorist bases in hostile countries. Those targets could be within the borders of extremely unstable nations, such as Afghanistan or Sudan. Such countries may have effective government only as far as the area around the capitol or in a few major cities, while the rest of the country remains a kind of badlands—lawless, extremist, and poverty-stricken. These are the regions one U.S. state department official termed "petri dishes" for terrorist cells, and the U.S. could preemptively strike training centers or meeting places if intelligence data warranted such an action. The preemptive strike policy could also be applied to individual or

and strike with unorthodox methods at American political and cultural symbols and population centers. In short, they're fighting dirty, but effectively. As atrocious as the attacks on New York City and Washington, D.C., were, their conception and execution were fraught with sinister brilliance. If global terrorists gain access to weapons of mass destruction, the possibilities will become even more frightening. Other asymmetric vulnerabilities exist in cyberspace, where

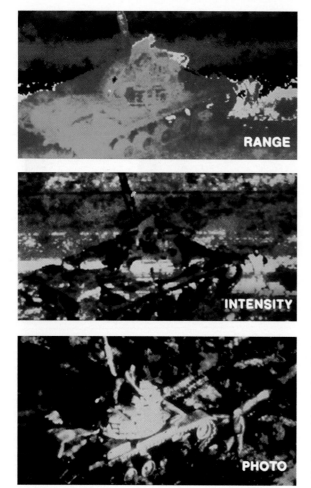

RANGE

INTENSITY

PHOTO

AIRBORNE SURVEILLANCE

Long a workhorse tactic, surveillance from above, whether by satellite or laser radar (above, in an actual photo and in images indicating range and intensity), has become even more important in the age of terrorism, when intelligence is the most potent weapon.

"rogue" nations, such as Iraq, that attempt to develop nuclear, biological, or chemical weapons.

The preemptive-strike doctrine will depend on the quality of information the U.S. can acquire about a potential hot spot. The military uses a wide range of radar, spy satellites, and reconnaissance planes to monitor specific localities and gather all manner of electronic communications for analysis. Ideally, all of this high-tech hardware would be able to ferret out threats all over the globe. But of course, in reality, it won't be able to anticipate every threat; the preemptive-strike doctrine relies heavily on first-rate intelligence, which won't always be available.

The U.S. can employ similar preventive tactics in cyberspace as well. A new breed of info-warriors sees the Internet as another front on the battlefield. A large part of their job is to secure computer networks against hackers who could attempt to cripple U.S. infrastructures via cyberspace.

Information technology will play other roles in 21st century military tactics as well. The U.S. is using the Internet to get tactical information to troops in the field more quickly. Commanders at Bagram Air Base in Afghanistan and at Central Command in Florida used a secret tactical Web page to help direct the war against the Taliban and al Qaeda. The page displayed battle maps indicating the locations of enemy and friendly

In Action

AWACS SENTRY

First deployed in 1977, the Airborne Warning and Control System made its combat debut in Operation Desert Storm in 1991. AWACS were among the first aircraft sent to the Persian Gulf during Operation Desert Shield, the buildup phase of the conflict. They immediately set up a 24-hour radar screen.

When the U.S. joined the battle, AWACS flew more than 400 missions and provided radar surveillance and control to more than 120,000 sorties. In addition to providing crucial, time-sensitive information on enemy activities, the AWACS assisted in 38 of the 40 air-to-air kills that U.S. pilots made during the war. All of the AWACS involved in the Gulf War returned to base unscathed.

forces, with continuous updates, and issued orders up and down the chain of command.

This fast network, in which any crucial information is only two clicks away, replaces the previous system that relied on paper maps and radio commmunications. Fast communication allows the U.S. military to effectively use intelligence against an enemy whose location may change within the hour or whose plan of attack has only just become evident. Networked communication also reduces the logistics of planning an operation, as all of the commanders involved can be briefed simultaneously, with visuals, while remaining in separate locations.

Speed is also critical for firing upon elusive targets. GPS navigation satellites can be used to home in on the target more precisely than ever, reducing the "sensor-to-shooter" time, the period between detection and firing, to minutes instead

AWACS SENTRY

With a Boeing 707 airframe and a four-man crew, the Airborne Warning and Control System, or AWACS, uses the 30-foot rotating radome mounted on its fuselage to identify an adversary's aircraft and jam enemy radar.

of hours. In line with these developments, the military is exploring hypersonic planes and guided missiles that fly at Mach speeds. DARPA test-fired a hypersonic projectile, basically a scaled-down model of a missile, in 2001. The small projectile was powered by a supersonic combustion scramjet engine burning hydrocarbon fuel, and it achieved speeds of Mach 7.1. Scramjets are engines that capture air to burn onboard fuel. Launched from a plane, for example, the scramjet engine takes over from a rocket engine (which provides the initial thrust) once the missile reaches hypersonic speed.

NETWORKED COMMAND

Specialist Jeremy Willey (above, right) works on a laptop at the U.S.'s Bagram Air Base in Afghanistan in April 2002. Commanders at Bagram used a secret tactical Web page to help direct the war against the Taliban and al Qaeda.

Hypersonic missiles, which might have a 400-mile range, can be powered all the way to the target, which improves their lethality against hardened or protected installations. And since the engine is operating, targeting information can be updated in mid-flight. Such a capability is important against targets like mobile Scud missile launchers that scurry into hiding moments after firing. Hypersonic missiles would be about seven times faster than conventional cruise missiles and cover a significantly greater area. Maximum flight time to any target would be about 10 minutes. These capabilities will be crucial to U.S. tactics against the 21st century's asymmetric adversaries.

On a larger scale, hypersonic technology is central to the Common Aero Vehicle (CAV) concept. The CAV would use the range and speed of intercontinental ballistic missiles to deliver non-

nuclear or conventional warheads. A CAV would be a gliding, 1,000-pound hypersonic "penetrator" that would be released within range of a target by a Minuteman III or similar missile after it re-entered the atmosphere. Flight time from Florida to a weapons-of-mass-destruction site near Basra, Iraq, for example, would be about 35 minutes. The CAV would approach the target at a velocity of about 10 times the speed of sound. Another delivery option for the CAV could be a military spaceplane that could deploy a reusable, sub-orbital mini-spaceplane, such as the Refly designed by Boeing. The Refly would carry two CAVs and would shorten flight time considerably.

Still another delivery possibility for the CAV are cruise missiles that loiter over an area of hostilities until they receive targeting instructions. Their final approach to the target would come from Special Forces troops on the ground, who would communicate GPS coordinates or provide laser targeting. Augmented by Central Intelligence Agency paramilitary operators and backed up by specially trained infantry units, these troops will be the tactical point of the spear in most 21st century operations. They will be the first to locate the adversary, call in fire support for strikes on enemy positions, and interrogate the survivors for further intelligence. The Special Forces troops will also train any surrogate forces—such as those of the Northern Alliance in Afghanistan—to fight side-by-side with U.S. soldiers or to maintain stability in a region following a conflict.

The most difficult theater for modern American soldiers has been, and will continue to be, the urban combat zone. In March 1999, the U.S. Marines staged a mock invasion of Northern California. In the battle for the city of Oakland, 70 percent of the attacking force was killed or wounded. As American troops learned in Somalia in 1993, threats in an urban environment can come from all directions. The urban combat theater may be the ultimate microcosm of asymmetric warfare.

For future encounters in unfriendly neighborhoods, the military has been developing its Military Operations on Urbanized Terrain (MOUT) combat doctrine. MOUT is designed to work with new technologies, like those involved in the Land Warrior program, to give soldiers the upper hand in urban settings.

The only other alternative is the approach Russia took in the battle for the city of Grozny during the Chechnya uprising of early 2000: They simply flattened it.

With a combination of state-of-the-art technology, improved intelligence, and sound fundamental tactics, the U.S. military can avoid such a ham-handed approach to the difficult combat theaters of the 21st century.

Spotlight CARBON BOMBS

In wars past, any army that wanted to knock out an enemy's electrical system simply bombed the adversary's power plants to piles of rubble. While effective, this tactic put pilots at risk from antiaircraft fire, and endangered civilian noncombatants who lived near the power plants.

A new tactic will target power plants with a carbon bomb. Carbon bombs are laser-guided, and at a predetermined point after they've been dropped, they split open, spinning and dispersing as many as 200 containers, each the size of a soda can. Inside each canister, a small explosive charge detonates, forcing the can to spring open and release a spool of carbon. The carbon spools from all 200 cans unravel and form a web (right), which descends to drape over power lines.

Highly conductive, the carbon web causes the power to surge and overload the circuits, forcing the plant to shut down. The resulting loss of power disrupts the enemy's communication systems and defense networks and becomes a source of significant inconvenience to the civilian population as well. The United States used carbon bombs during the Persian Gulf War and in its interventions in the Balkans in the late 1990s.

READY FOR DUTY

TERRORISM IS HARDLY NEW, BUT THE ATROCITY OF SEPTEMBER 11 GAVE IT A REVOLUTIONARY FORM AND FOREVER CHANGED THE TACTICS AND THEATERS OF WARFARE IN THE 21ST CENTURY.

SEPTEMBER 11 ATTACKS

On September 11, 2001, terrorists hijacked four airliners out of northeastern airports, flying two of them into the World Trade Center in New York City (opposite) and one into the Pentagon in Washington, D.C. (above). The fourth plane crashed in rural Pennsylvania.

TERRORISM MAY BE AS OLD AS WARFARE ITSELF. In 600 B.C., warriors used terror tactics such as poisoning a city's water supply with toxic herbs. During the French and Indian War, British troops distributed smallpox-infected blankets to Native Americans, killing hundreds.

In 1864, rogue Confederate soldiers based in Canada terrorized the community of St. Albans, Vermont. Their raid spread fear through northern communities from Maine to Montana. In November of the same year, a handful of Confederate terrorists rode a train into New York City and set fires to a total of 19 hotels and theatrical venues. The raids were not terribly damaging, but they demonstrated that the North was vulnerable to guerrilla attacks.

PALESTINIAN ISLAMIC JIHAD

During a rally in Gaza City on June 1, 2001, members of the militant Palestinian Islamic Jihad, which has carried out some of the most deadly acts of terrorism in history, vow to continue their fight against Israel.

By mid-2002, there were 10 established terrorist groups willing and able to use suicide attacks against their perceived enemies. They included the Islam Resistance Movement (Hamas) and the Palestinian Islamic Jihad of the Israeli occupied territories; Hezbullah of Lebanon; the Egyptian Islamic Jihad (EIJ) and Gamaya Islamiya (Islamic Group—IG) of Egypt; the Armed Islamic Group (GIA) of Algeria; Barbar Khalsa International (BKI) of India; the Liberation Tigers of Tamil Eelam (LTTE) of Sri Lanka; the Kurdistan Worker's Party (PKK) of

Turkey; and al Qaeda, the network originally based in Afghanistan and organized by Saudi exile Osama bin Laden.

Currently, the United States is focusing on al Qaeda, but that doesn't mean the others don't pose threats. Some of them may be attempting to acquire nuclear weapons. While a nuclear bomb is a sophisticated weapon, there have been college and high school students who have figured out how to design one. Plans for nuclear weapons are available on the Internet. The obstacle to terrorist cells' efforts to go nuclear is not so much know-how as materials.

If the terrorists could get their hands on plutonium or enriched uranium, they could probably enlist a team of nuclear scientists to develop a bomb in the 1-kiloton range. Despite what nuclear-power advocates say, nuclear reactors

HAMAS

In the Jabalya refugee camp in Gaza, three Palestinian schoolboys play with a soccer ball in front of graffiti praising two former leaders of Hamas's military wing who were killed in battles with Israeli armed forces.

can provide enough atomic material for a bomb. And it takes less than 18 pounds of plutonium, or 55 pounds of highly enriched uranium, to build a nuclear bomb. Such materials circulate by the ton in the world of civilian nuclear commerce. Al Qaeda has attempted to acquire nuclear material and nuclear-weapon design information. All of this begs the question: Is this a serious threat?

The International Atomic Energy Agency currently recommends that nations improve their protection of civilian and military nuclear materials both at nuclear power plants and while the material is in transit. But it might be impossible to secure all of the nuclear materials in the world. Since the fall of the Soviet Union in 1991, Russia and its former Soviet satellite states have had a surplus of both materials and hungry, out-

of-work nuclear scientists. The U.S. has spent millions of dollars to help the former communist nations keep their nuclear houses in order—and to find work for the scientists.

No one in the U.S. knows exactly how much fissile material the Soviet Union made or how secure its storage facilities are. But there are confirmed instances of Russian nuclear materials turning up on the black market. The biggest problem for terrorists may be getting the materials into the country—so long as radiation detectors are in place in all ports of entry.

AIRPORT SECURITY

Heavily armed national guardsmen like Sgts. Peter Bellegarde (right) and Jason Perry provided additional security in airport terminals across the United States following the terrorist attacks of September 11, 2001.

Terrorists may also resort to so-called "dirty" bombs, radioactive bombs that, while nowhere near as powerful as nukes, would still make a formidable instrument of terror. And they are considerably easier to build, requiring only an explosive—readily available on the U.S. black market—and any kind of radioactive material. Terrorists could get the necessary material from a nuclear reactor, or from indus-

try or medical facilities, or even from landfills.

A dirty bomb would cause destruction identical to that of a conventional bomb of the same size but would leave its ground-zero area uninhabitable for weeks, months, or years. Unless a strong wind were blowing, a dirty bomb wouldn't create much fallout, and, as we've said, it would have nothing like the force of a proper nuclear weapon. But a tall building in downtown Manhattan would make a perfect target for a dirty bomb. All the terrorist would need is a suitcase or a van to transport the bomb.

At the same time, some terrorist organizations are pursuing biological and chemical weapons programs. Instructions for how to pro-

RADIATION DETECTOR
Developed by the Lawrence Berkeley National Laboratory, this hand-held, battery-powered device could foil terrorists attempting to transport radioactive materials.

duce weapons-grade chemical and biological agents are readily available on the Internet, and terrorists could disperse them through the mail—or in crop-duster planes.

So what tactics can the U.S. employ to combat terrorism in the asymmetric theater of its own homeland? It can distribute nuclear, biological, and chemical detectors to police, customs agents, and airport security guards. The FBI and the CIA and the new Department of Homeland Security can widen and enhance their intelligence networks, and their cooperation, and acquire agents fluent in Arabic and Farsi, to name

two languages relevant to global terrorism.

Perhaps the greatest lesson of Vietnam is that getting involved in another country's business is a risky proposition, one the U.S. can only undertake with overwhelming force and eyes wide open. And the U.S. can't afford to win the war but lose the peace, as it did in the Gulf War, trouncing Iraqi forces in short order, but leaving Saddam Hussein in power, where he remains a thorn in America's side a decade later.

As President Abraham Lincoln and Gen. Ulysses S. Grant knew, the U.S. must achieve total victory but also treat its enemies with a measure of dignity and respect, especially after the hostilities cease. War reparations from the Treaty of Versailles so crippled Germany's economy that it gave rise to Adolf Hitler. After World War II, Gen. George C. Marshall outlined the Marshall Plan to rebuild the wrecked nations of Europe, regardless of which side they were on. Today, Germany has the strongest

In Action

HOMELAND SECURITY

Americans have made several adjustments in response to the terrorist attacks of September 2001, not least of which is an increased sensitivity on the part of individual citizens to possible threats.

Slightly more than two months after the September 11 attacks, travelers on American Airlines Flight 63 demonstrated this new vigilance in stirring fashion. During the flight from Paris to Miami, a passenger attempted to detonate explosives he

had smuggled onto the plane in his sneakers. Noticing his attempts to light the explosives, flight attendants and passengers jumped the would-be terrorist, creating a melee that spilled into the aisle. Among the passengers involved was the 6' 8", 225-pound Kwame James, who played basketball at the University of Evansville. Said James, "It took me and three or four other guys just to hold him down. He almost seemed possessed."

Spotlight   TACTICS IN AFGHANISTAN

Afghanistan has long been regarded as a kind of LaBrea Tar Pit for would-be invaders. From the English in 1839 to the Soviet Union in the 1980s, invading armies have met with rugged terrain and fierce resistance, but little success in repeated attempts to conquer the Middle Eastern nation. Experts pointed out these failed efforts as a warning to the United States before it mounted its October 2001 campaign against the Taliban, which was sheltering Osama bin Laden, alleged organizer of the September 11 terrorist attacks on New York City and Washington, D.C.

So how did the U.S. achieve its successes in such a famously difficult theater? The answer is twofold: In the early stages of the war, the American tactics consisted of deploying two or three dozen Special Operations troops to command regiments of Afghan soldiers, who were doing most of the fighting on the ground. In addition to their roles as commanders, the Special Ops soldiers used satellite technology to call in air strikes, which proved immensely effective. With such potent bombs as the 15,000-pound Daisy Cutter (above) and the 2.5-ton GBU-28 blowing football-field-size craters in the earth, the air strikes utterly destroyed Taliban trenches, bunkers, and fortifications on the ground.

After several weeks of effective airstrikes, the U.S. shifted its tactics to assume better control of activities on the ground and limit the number of Taliban and al Qaeda escapees. In this phase, the U.S. used units of 100 to 300 of its elite troops, with a handful of interpreters, to conduct lightning-quick raids on al Qaeda hide-outs. This approach often involved U.S. soldiers rooting through individual Afghan homes in search of al Qaeda operatives, or probing deep into the nation's vast mountain ranges. It was a cat-and-mouse game that often ended in futility, but it was a far sight better than the Soviet performance in the 1980s, or the English effort in the 19th century.

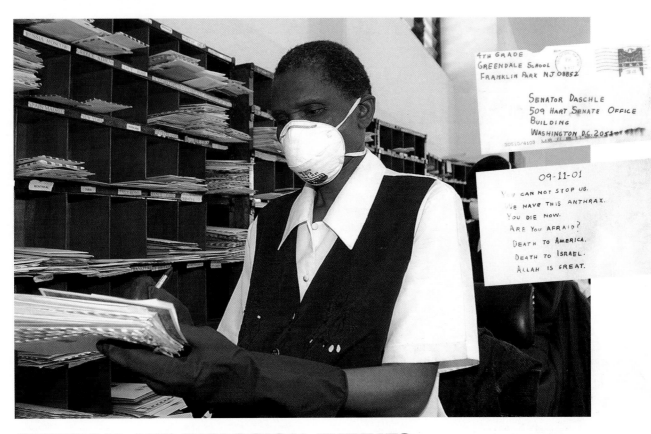

CHEMICAL AND BIOLOGICAL THREATS

In the weeks after the September 11 terrorist attacks, Senate Majority Leader Tom Daschle, among others, received letters (inset) laced with weapons-grade anthrax; the perpetrators of these attacks, which endangered postal workers (above) as much as their intended victims, have yet to be apprehended. Five people, including two mail processors in Washington, D.C., were killed by anthrax inhalation, and dozens tested positive for exposure to the substance.

economy in Europe and is one of America's closest allies. Gen. Douglas MacArthur vowed to rebuild Japan after Hiroshima and Nagasaki, and today the Land of the Rising Sun has the world's second-strongest economy, behind that of the U.S. Neither of the former bitter adversaries poses a threat to America.

While George W. Bush has said he opposes "nation building," the U.S. must participate in something quite a bit like it if America is to wipe out terrorism entirely. It won't do to simply destroy terrorist targets in Afghanistan and then abandon the country to its former chaos. This would be not only morally questionable, it would also create more terrorists in the wake of the invasion. The U.S. must attend to the economies and the stability of such nations after

it completes its military missions. If terrorism and poverty go hand in hand, terrorism and prosperity are like oil and water—the relative affluence of the September 11 hijackers notwithstanding. If young men in these "petri-dish" nations had food on their tables and roofs over their heads, they would be highly unlikely to turn their gripes into acts of terrorism.

The current U.S. defense budget is slightly more than $342 billion; $40 billion, or 12 percent of that budget, could provide water, sanitation, education, and basic nutrition to every developing nation in the world. Such an act of charity may be a pipe dream, but it's worth keeping in mind because, ultimately, all of our high-tech weapons and all of our highly trained soldiers can't protect all of us from random acts of terrorism.

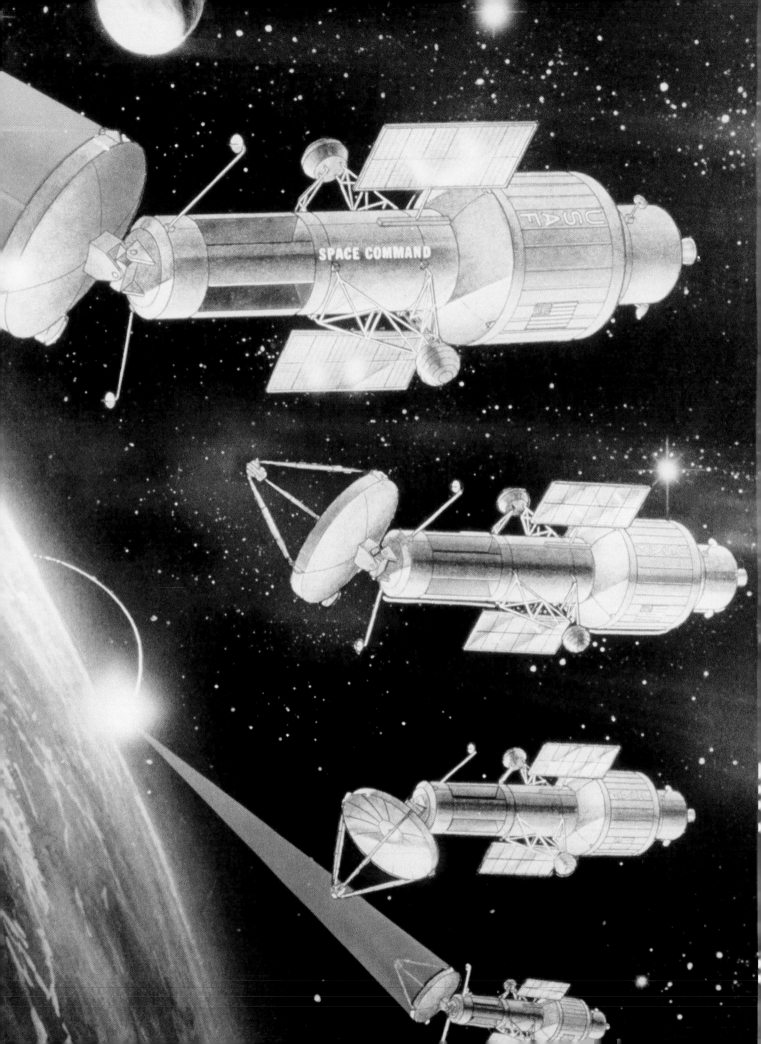

[TACTICS]
CUTTING EDGE

U.S. MILITARY ANALYSTS ARE DEVELOPING TACTICS AND TECHNOLOGIES TO DEAL WITH AN ARRAY OF THREATS IN THE 21ST CENTURY, FROM BOMB-PROOF BUNKERS TO THE ASYMMETRY OF TERRORISM, TO CYBERWAR.

SOMEDAY IN THE NOT-SO-DISTANT FUTURE, the President of the United States could receive during his daily intelligence briefing the stunning news that a hostile force is on the verge of using a deadly biological agent against the United States. Even more disturbing, his advisors might tell him, is that the enemy launch facility is buried in a bunker 100 feet underground. At that depth, the bunker would be impervious to conventional weapons—even the deadly, air-sucking thermobaric bombs deployed against the Tora Bora caves of Afghanistan in 2001-02 would be useless. The only option would be to use a ground-penetrating mini-nuclear weapon that would destroy the facility and the toxic agent in the same nuclear fireball. On the bright side of this considerably dark scenario is that the nuclear blast

SPACE-LASER/ GBU-28
The U.S. is currently developing a space-based laser (opposite, in artist's concept) that could hit targets both in space and on the ground; the 2.5-ton, laser-guided GBU-28 (above) is famous as a "bunker buster."

167

The Other Side

GLOBAL TERRORISM

Sadly, as the 21st century progresses, citizens of the United States will have to adjust to a new fact of life, one that much of the rest of the world has lived with for decades: At any moment, the fabric of Americans' daily lives can be torn asunder by a terrorist attack.

Previously, terrorists targeted American interests abroad, such as embassies or military bases. But the first attack on New York City's World Trade Center, in February 1993, was a sign that terrorists were homing in on the U.S. mainland. The second, of course, was the worst attack on U.S. soil in the nation's history.

There are several agents of global terrorism, but perhaps the most prominent is the al Qaeda network, which sponsored the September 11 attacks. Al Qaeda wages what the State Department has termed asymmetric warfare, and the defenses against such warfare are similarly asymmetric, including freezing the assets that fund the terrorists, gathering intelligence on al Qaeda cells, which are myriad and scattered over the globe, improving surveillance technology, and coordinating the U.S.-based agencies responsible for dealing with terrorist threats. The enemy is determined and elusive, but with the proper vigilance, he can be defeated like any other.

would be contained underground, reducing or even eliminating the fallout that could kill any civilian population surrounding the target.

This is the military's nightmare future scenario, the solution to which can only be described as the lesser of two evils. There is even a sliver of doubt—which, in this context, may as well be a chasm—that the "mini-nuke" option would work as planned. Some physicists believe that any missile would disintegrate from force of impact long before reaching the underground target, and that the resulting nuclear explosion would probably spew a plume of radiation out through the entrance hole like a Roman candle in a fireworks display, killing tens of thousands of people on the surface.

While the U.S. and Russia are reducing the number of intercontinental nuclear missiles that threatened to end the world during the Cold War, the Bush Administration's decision to resume the production of plutonium pits in 2020 serves notice that the nuclear option is still in play. Plutonium pits are nuclear weapons parts that contain the hollow shells of nuclear materials, and their continued production assures us that future presidents will be able to use mini-nukes—bombs with a yield of less than 10 kilotons—in any such nightmare scenario.

The Defense Department estimates that there are 10,000 underground bunkers in the world today, and their number grows daily. The rationale for their construction is simple: To avoid spy satellites and precision-guided missiles, go underground. "The North Koreans have turned their country into a big piece of Swiss cheese," says noted military analyst John Pike, director of GlobalSecurity.org. "Iraq and North Korea have tunnels that would put Tora Bora to shame. It's a real no-kidding problem."

Analysts debate whether or not any future U.S. president would be able to cross the nuclear threshold, but they have no doubt that the military would make every effort to offer a conventional solution. To that end, military brass will lobby for

ASYMMETRIC WARFARE

A new era of warfare dawned on September 11, 2001, when terrorists rammed two hijacked airliners into the World Trade Center towers in New York City.

the construction of bigger and bigger bombs with ever more massive payloads.

This trend began in the Gulf War and continued in Afghanistan in 2001-02, when the U.S. Air Force dropped bombs roughly the size of small cars on Taliban and al Qaeda strongholds. Among these bunker busters were the 2.5-ton, laser-guided GBU-28 and its cousin, the GPS-guided GBU-37B. Both bombs are essentially modified artillery designed to penetrate 20 feet of concrete before exploding.

The U.S. also pounded Afghanistan with the 15,000-pound behemoth officially called BLU-82, also known as the Daisy Cutter or Big Blue. The Daisy Cutter is too big for the bomb-bay doors on most aircraft, so it had to be pushed out the back of an MC-130 cargo plane flying over Afghanistan. The largest conventional weapon in the Air Force's arsenal, the massive bomb collapsed Taliban trenches and fortifications around Mazar-i-Sharif and played an instrumental role in the defeat of Taliban forces.

In addition to bunkers, the tactical conundrums of the future could involve a nuclear threat from a rogue nation or, even more frighteningly, a terrorist cell. The rogue-nation threat provides the rationale for development of a national missile-defense shield. In this system, which remains in the conceptual phase, a network of advanced sensors would detect the launch of a nuclear missile at its source. Within minutes, interceptor missiles would destroy the threat. Hitting a bullet with another bullet, however, has proved difficult in practice, and experts estimate that the cost of a missile shield program would reach tens of billions of dollars.

Terrorist cells, or nation states that use terrorist tactics, present a more immediate threat. Symbolic landmarks and population centers are the most inviting targets for these adversaries. The most horrific example of these threats—which military strategists have dubbed asymmetric warfare—is the September 11, 2001, terrorist attack on New York City's World Trade Center and the Pentagon in Washington, D.C. As everyone knows all too well, terrorists hijacked commercial airliners and used them as guided missiles. Another example of asymmetric warfare was the terrorist attack on the *U.S.S. Cole* in Yemen on October 12, 2000. Two men in a rubber dinghy loaded with explosives killed 17 U.S. sailors and injured 39 in a suicide attack that disabled the *Cole*. The most chilling notion in the asymmetric scenario? Military analysts agree that it is easier and cheaper to sneak a nuclear bomb into a U.S. harbor aboard a nondescript freighter than it would be to develop an intercontinental missile program.

In asymmetric warfare, the enemy doesn't wear

GPS

The militarization of space already includes weapons that use Global Positioning System navigation satellites for targeting. Technologically advanced adversaries of the 21st century will target each other's space assets.

a uniform and may be indistinguishable from the general population. He may have few or no physical assets that can be attacked. A large-scale military response may be useless against a pin-prick terrorist attacker, like taking a sledgehammer on a picnic to keep the gnats at bay. Small, fast-moving special-ops units will be the force of choice in asymmetric warfare.

A key technology in this emerging form of combat are spy satellites. While satellites can already produce photographs of objects on Earth that show tiny details, a feature called hyperspectral imaging will sharpen their intelligence-gathering capabilities even more. Hyperspectral imaging is capable of differentiating between the slightest variations in color. Assuming the existence of a comparative database, a spy satellite could detect a suspect ship at sea and identify its country of origin by its paint signature, a procedure that Satlantic, a Halifax-based company, is currently

developing. Hyperspectral imaging has already made traditional camouflage obsolete, since it can easily distinguish between a camouflaged tank and overhanging trees.

Control of the high ground is always a prime combat objective, and since space now represents the ultimate high ground (so to speak), the military jealously protects its space assets. For all intents and purposes, the U.S. currently dominates space, as it has long relied on space satellites for communications and intelligence gathering. The militarization of space could soon include weapons systems that use GPS navigation satellites for targeting. The military brass is well aware that any technologically advanced adversary would target U.S. space assets first, since their destruction would leave the U.S. military essentially blind. While a nuclear explosion in space would certainly impact any technology positioned there, it could be a ham-handed approach that runs the risk of damaging the space assets of friends as well as foes. A better alternative might be a ground-based laser, rumored to be in development in China. This weapon could target individual satellites, and its rumored existence hastens

Spotlight CYBERWAR

If China ever decides to retake Taiwan, its first hostile step toward that goal may not be to fire a missile into Taipei, the Taiwanese capital, but to unleash a computer virus that would cripple Taiwan's information infrastructure. Such a virus could disrupt military communications, power grids, train transport, and banking networks, to name a few systems.

Of course, Taiwan is hardly alone in its vulnerability. A modern nation's dependency on computer networks means that it must make protecting itself from viruses, worms, and other cyberthreats a top priority. The United States and many other countries now have "infowarrior" detachments (left) whose role is to fight bloodless battles against enemy hackers whom they may never positively identify.

Further complicating matters is the fact that the Internet can function as a modern-day parallel to the United States's Navajo Code Talkers, who made U.S. radio communications secure during World War II with a code based on the Navajo language. (The Japanese never cracked the Navajo code.) Instead of an arcane language unfamiliar to the enemy, covert message senders on the Internet use extremely complex encryption that's all but unbreakable. With a technique called steganography, Internet users can hide messages within, say, the pixels of a seemingly innocuous photograph posted as an item for sale on e-Bay. Only the sender and the recipient would possess the software key to unlock the missive. Computer security experts are developing methods for detecting the use of steganography—but such is the state of this shadowy world that they are unsure if they are ahead of or behind the curve.

the need for American military spaceplanes that could quickly replace destroyed satellites.

The U.S., which already operates a ground-based laser capable of hitting targets in space, is planning to develop a space-based laser that could hit targets both in space and on the ground. Yet, a space-based laser would be ineffective against what military analysts currently perceive as the most significant threat in the world: weapons of mass destruction housed in underground bunkers. War gamers recently witnessed one potential solution to this problem: "rods from God," uranium-enriched hypervelocity guided rods that could be launched from space and would create giant craters upon impact.

The greatest risk for military minds, however, is that in preparing for future conflicts, they produce self-fulfilling prophecies. In 1923, the Japanese Imperial Navy decided that the United States was its biggest potential adversary and geared the development of its naval forces accordingly. Eighteen years later, Japan was fighting a losing war with the U.S.

The U.S. will have to make similar choices about its future, and only time will determine the wisdom of those decisions.

PHOTO CREDITS

Cover:
Sarah Underhill, Soldier Systems Center.

Back cover:
Top, AFP/CORBIS; left, John B. Carnett/*Popular Science;* right, LCPL Antonio J. Vega/JCCC.

1, AFP/CORBIS; 2-3, AFP/CORBIS; 6, AFP/CORBIS; 10-11, Lockheed Martin; 12-13, Sygma/CORBIS; 14, U.S. Air Force; 15, SuperStock; 16, George Hall/CORBIS; 17, Rabih Moghrabi/AFP/CORBIS; 19, SuperStock; 20-21, Boeing; 22, Boeing; 23, Lockheed Martin; 24, Lockheed Martin; 26, Lockheed Martin; 27, Boeing; 29, Boeing; 30, U.S. Air Force; 31, Boeing; 32, John B. Carnett/*Popular Science;* 33, Boeing; 34, John B. Carnett/*Popular Science;* 36-37, AP; 38-39, Attar Maher/CORBIS SYGMA; 40-41, AFP/CORBIS; 42, CORBIS; 43, PH1 Ted Banks/JCCC; 44-45, SuperStock; 46-47, Michael Lemke/JCCC; 48, SPC Christina Ann Horne/JCCC; 49, Leif Skoogfors/CORBIS; 50-51, Courtesy of General Dynamics (2); 52, John B. Carnett/*Popular Science* (2); 53, Sean P. Quinn/JCCC; 54-55, 1st LT. Tony Vitello/JCCC; 56, Boeing; 57, John B. Carnett/*Popular Science;* 58-59, Courtesy of General Dynamics (4); 60, Boeing; 61, Courtesy of General Dynamics; 62, Space and Naval Warfare Systems Center, San Diego; 63, iRobot; 64-65, SuperStock; 66-67, PH1 Ted Banks/JCCC; 68-69, SuperStock (2); 70, PHAN Tina R. Lamb/JCCC; 71, Luciano Mellace/Reuters; 72-73, PHC Lawrence B. Foster/JCCC; 74-75, Seth Rothman/AFP/CORBIS (2); 76, Mark Farmer; 77, Lockheed Martin; 78, LCPL Antonio J. Vega/JCCC; 81, PH2 Shane McCoy/JCCC; 82, Courtesy of QinetiQ; 83, NAVSEA; 84, NAVSEA; 85, Lockheed Martin; 86, Concept Artwork Courtesy of Northrop Grumman (2); bottom, AP; 88-89, NAVSEA; 89, top, Total Ship Systems Engineering Program Naval Postgraduate School (3); bottom, Courtesy of Naval Undersea Warfare Center; 90-91, Leif Skoogfors/CORBIS; 92-93, Jim Hollander/AFP/CORBIS; 94, Leif Skoogfors/CORBIS; 95, Kevin Fleming/CORBIS; 96-97, PH1 Arlo L. Abrahamson/JCCC; 98, Aaron Favila/AP; 99, SGT. John Vannucci/JCCC; 100-101, JCCC; 101, right, SGT Ronald A. Mitchell/JCCC; 102, Precision Remotes; 103, BAE Systems; 104-105, Brooks Kraft/CORBIS SYGMA; 106, Courtesy of ATK (2); 107, Textron Systems; 108-109, Metal Storm Limited; 110, Sarah Underhill, Soldier Systems Center; 111, John B. Carnett/*Popular Science;* 112, John B. Carnett/*Popular Science;* 113, Sarah Underhill, Soldier Systems Center; 115, top, Dr. F. J. Pompei/MIT Media Lab; bottom, SuperStock; 116-117, Courtesy of Kirtland Air Force Base (2); 118-119, Leif Skoogfors/CORBIS; 120-121, AFP/CORBIS; 122, Pool/Reuters/TimePix; 123, Bob Daugherty/AP; 124, top, Bettmann/CORBIS; bottom, SPC Robin A. Quander/JCCC; 125, Kraft Brooks/CORBIS; 126, SSGT Larry A. Simmons/JCCC; 127, Jens Meyer/AP; 128, Courtesy of Thales Acoustics (2); 129, LCPL Matthew J. Decker/JCCC; 130, Brooks Kraft/CORBIS SYGMA; 131, Jill Connelly/AP; 132, top, Photonics Division of Intevac; bottom, Sarah Underhill, Soldier Systems Center; 133, Sarah Underhill, Soldier Systems Center; 134-135, Courtesy of Montague Corporation (2); 136, Sarah Underhill, Soldier Systems Center; 137, John B. Carnett/*Popular Science;* 138, Sarah Underhill, Soldier Systems Center; 139, John B. Carnett/*Popular Science;* 140, Sarah Underhill, Soldier Systems Center; 141, John B. Carnett/*Popular Science* (3); 142-143, John B. Carnett/*Popular Science* (2); 144, DARPA; 145, Sarah Underhill, Soldier Systems Center; 146-147, John Frassanito & Associates, Inc.; 148-149, J. Scott Applewhite/AP; 150-151, Peter Turnley/CORBIS (2); 152, Tim Shaffer/Reuters/CORBIS; 153, Ralph Orlowski/Reuters/CORBIS; 154, Lockheed Martin (3); 155, Mark Farmer; 156, Todd Pitman/AP; 157, AFP/CORBIS; 158, Reuters/CORBIS; 159, Patrick Sison/AP; 160, Adel Hana/AP; 161, Greg Baker/AP; 162, Joel Page/AP; 163, Reuters/CORBIS; 164, George Frey/TimePix; 165, Antony Njuguna/Reuters/CORBIS; 166, Courtesy of FAS; 167, Manuel M. Chavez/AP; 169, Carmen Taylor/AP; 170, Boeing; 171, Dennis Brack/TimePix.

INDEX